Praise for *Make Love Work for You:*

'The style is refreshingly down-to-earth. It is written movingly and wittily and the author has kept a light, readable tone throughout the book, leaving the reader in no doubt about the serious professional expertise and knowledge that underpins the advice. Anne Nicholls is supportive to the reader but punchily confrontational at the same time. I love this combination of warmth and bluntness.'

Gael Lindenfield, author of *Assert Yourself, Self Esteem, Emotional Confidence* and many other titles

'This is a well-crafted book. Anne Nicholls speaks directly to her reader, in a style that is refreshingly free from therapeutic jargon. Her book will be an immediately practical and useful tool for anyone wanting to repair or enhance their personal relationships.'

Dr Ian Stewart, co-author of *TA Today* and *Personality Adaptations*

MAKE LOVE WORK FOR YOU

A toolkit for finding happiness in your relationship

MAKE LOVE WORK FOR YOU

A toolkit for finding happiness in your relationship

Anne Nicholls

PIATKUS

Copyright © 2002 by Anne Nicholls

First published in 2002 by
Judy Piatkus (Publishers) Limited
5 Windmill Street
London W1T 2JA
e-mail: info@piatkus.co.uk

The moral right of the author has been asserted

A catalogue record for this book is available from the British Library

ISBN 0 7499 2332 6

Text design by Tracy Timson
Edited by Barbara Kiser

This book has been printed on paper manufactured with respect for the environment using wood from managed sustainable resources

Typeset by Phoenix Photosetting, Chatham, Kent
Printed and bound in Italy by Chromo Litho Ltd

Dedication

To my wonderful husband, Stan Nicholls, who has made learning about relationships such fun.

And to Helen Inman, who, with Tony, Jesse and Rebecca, is a constant source of tea, sympathy and support.

Contents

Your Safety Net   81

You and Me

Checking Out the Opposition

If you're unsure whether this will be a good relationship for you, or if you tend to blame yourself when things go wrong, here are some useful tools for checking out potential partners

15. Silent Signals

If you're not sure how to flirt with someone or whether you should, Silent Signals will help you give – and get – the response you're after

16. The Detective

Have partners reacted in ways you don't understand? The Detective shows you a way to check out what's going on for them – and what you can do about it

One Date at a Time

Have you ever been unsure at the start of a relationship? These tools can help you manage the first stages comfortably

17. The Date Menu

The Date Menu is useful if you've ever felt at a loss when trying to find decent partners, or uncomfortable on first dates

18. The Safe Pace

Have you ever found yourself diving in at the deep end only to come to grief? The Safe Pace is a way to maintain comfort and security with new people

Together At Last

Acknowledgements

I'd like to thank all my trainers, particularly Ian Stewart, Adrienne Lee and Tony Tilney; all the great people I trained with, especially Marilyn Wright, Tricia White, Mark Widdowson and Judith Partridge; my supervisors and therapists Mo Felton, Gwynn Phelps and Simon Gubb; and all the people with whom I work at Solihull MIND, especially Angela Leake, Moira Oldroyd and Simon Painter. They've all been helpful and supportive. Special thanks to Helen Inman, who has so kindly read the manuscript and offered useful comments.

Any inaccuracies are my own.

Thanks also to all my clients, who have taught me such a lot.

Introduction

Do you want a more satisfying love-life?

Jim and Carly fired accusations at each other like bullets at their divorce hearing. Neither of them understood how they'd got there. They'd been so much in love – until it all went wrong. Now they were bitter, confused and disillusioned. Other people were happy. Why weren't they? It all seemed so unfair.

Meanwhile, Emma was saying tearfully, 'Every time I think I've met the right man I end up getting hurt. I can't see myself ever finding real love.'

Have you ever felt that way? I know I used to. So have the men and women who come to me for counselling. They may be successful and good-looking or they may believe they're life's rejects, but the one thing they've got in common is that they're unhappy. 'Why me?' and 'If only' are themes I deal with daily.

You might think I'd be miserable in my work, but I'm not. What I see is not the despair but the joy to come. I see people facing up to their problems and finding out how to make things right. I see the wonder on people's faces as they realise they *can* untangle the knots in their love-lives. Some of these people are making a new start. Others are revitalising relationships that had been frustrating or painful. When they reach the safe harbour of the love they've always wanted, they wave me goodbye. Some invite me to their weddings or send cards to tell me how happy they are now.

I know how they feel. I wasn't born knowing how to make relationships work. 'Love' wasn't on the timetable at school. I too had a long apprenticeship in heartache, but when I finally learned how to solve my emotional problems I found happiness in a wonderful marriage. I didn't know it, but all I'd needed were the right tools. Once I had them, how could I keep them to myself?

A good relationship enriches your life. It fills you with confidence, shelters you when things go wrong and provides comfort and security. A poor relationship, on the other hand, can range from terrifying to simply dull. But good relationships don't just happen. If you were fixing a car, you'd need the right tools and the knowledge to put it all together. It's the same thing with relationships. Perhaps, like Emma, things have never worked out for you. Perhaps, like Jim and Carly, you've had relationships that start out bright and hopeful but end in disaster.

But it doesn't have to be that way. With the right tools and the knowledge of how to use them, you too can build the relationship you want.

So what are these tools? They're principles used by therapists and counsellors all over the world as part of the therapeutic process, simple techniques that hundreds of thousands of people have proved are effective in solving everyday relationship problems. I've gathered them in this book, so that in essence it's a bit like a toolbox you can open up when you need to.

For example, if you've ever felt rejected or overwhelmed by a partner, your **Personal Safety Zone** will show you how to find and set the limits that feel right for you. Or you may have wondered if you've somehow been setting yourself up to fail. The **Sabotage Squelch** is just what you need to identify and overcome that problem. If you've been wondering how come you always seem to pick the wrong partner, the **Type Spotter** will show you how to check if the next one is right for you. The **Trap Map**, on the other hand, is one of a battery of techniques you can use to avoid common problems in the relationships you have. These tools originate in a wide variety of therapeutic approaches. They're practical and effective. They've certainly worked for my clients – and for me.

You can learn to operate them too. For every problem there's a solution, even problems like the ones below. How many of them do you identify with?

He won't make a commitment.
Any partner's better than being left on the shelf.
I try and try but I can't make it work.
I always pick the wrong people.
Men/women don't want the same things I do.
It's all his fault.
It's all her fault.
It's all my fault.
All men are bastards and all women are cows.
There's nobody decent out there.
I never meet the right person.
He/she will change once we're together.
I always get dumped.
All the good ones are already taken.
I've been hurt so badly I'm too scared to try again.
You can't trust anybody.
Who'd want me?
One-night stands are safer.
If I let anyone get close they'll hurt me.

You may recognise several of these problems, or perhaps yours have been different. You will know because when it comes down to it, you are the expert on you. You know more about yourself than anybody else does. After all, you're the only person who's ever had exactly your experiences. You're the one who lives in your body and through your senses. Your problems affect you in your own unique way. You know what you'd like to be changed and what would feel right for you.

You're also the only person who's been in every single one of your relationships. The common thread that runs through them is you, and that's good news because it gives you more control from now on. Even the most timid person can safely learn how to have the power to do things differently and get a better outcome. From picking the right people to finding the courage to get more of what you want, there are tools that can help – if you apply them.

Whether you're in a relationship you'd like to improve or you're not in one at all, I invite you to consider whether what you've been doing so far has been working for you. If you keep on doing it, is that going to change things? Or is it likely to get you more of the same?

As things are, you're looking for a new approach or you wouldn't be reading this book. Are you willing to open yourself up to new possibilities? Possibilities where you can let go of old pain and move to a more comfortable future with someone whose love, far from hurting, will uplift and nurture you? Isn't it worth at least considering using new tools to cut through those old problems and head into a fresh, more rewarding way of loving?

Here's some more good news. You're only 50 per cent of any relationship. There are two of you in it, not just you. If you've been taking all the blame for everything, you can stop. If you've been blaming the other person for everything, you can learn how to find your own power and use it to change what needs to be changed.

Each of the chapters in this book identifies one particular problem or an aspect of that problem. Each of them gives you the tools you need to sort it out. The first section, 'You and Your Needs', shows you how you can overcome past hurts and present fears, and most of all keep yourself safe so you have more confidence in your dealings with other people. 'You and Me', the second section, shows you how you can find the right person, make good choices, break old habits and put new, positive patterns in place. 'Together at Last' deals with the two of you building a better relationship together so that you can achieve and keep the love you want. At the end of the book you'll find a list of useful resources, from groups and counsellors to books and videos.

This book isn't a substitute for therapy. If you feel your problems are so deep you could 'go crazy' and hurt yourself or someone else, it's a good idea to seek help from your GP or a counsellor straight away. The tools on offer will still be here when you're ready for them. And they *will* work if you apply them. You *can* find the love you want, and *Make Love Work For You* can show you how.

I wish you as much pleasure and fulfilment in your relationships as you can imagine – and more!

You and Your Needs

Your Personal Safety Zone

Have you been hurt in love? Here's how you can keep yourself safe in relationships

Your **Personal Safety Zone** is made up of three smaller, interlocking tools:

The **Safe Boundary Framework** holds it together.

The **'Old Rules' Eraser** eradicates negative behavioural principles and lays a foundation for positive and assertive behaviours.

The **Sabotage Squelch** identifies and eliminates underlying beliefs which brought painful results, and replaces them with optimism and confidence.

1

—

The Safe Boundary Framework

Do you fear rejection or being swallowed up in relationships? Here's the first step towards protecting yourself

Love doesn't have to hurt

Few of us have love-lives that turn out as we'd hoped. You may have found heartache instead of joyous companionship. Maybe you've been betrayed, bullied or neglected. Alternatively, you may have cut and run before you got in too deep.

You might not have seen it coming. Even if you did, you may have hoped against hope that if only you could hang on long enough to weather the storm, everything would turn out right this time.

But it doesn't have to be this way! Instead of feeling lost and at sea, you can start to take control of your love-life. You can learn tactics to find and keep the right partner. However hopeless a case you may have thought you were, you *can* develop relationship skills – if someone shows you how.

It's not magic. In any activity there are tools you need to know how to use, and love is no exception. If other people can learn and apply emotional tools that maximise their chance of happiness, so can you!

Whether you're gathering confidence to get back into the dating game or whether you're in a relationship that's not what you hoped it would be, you don't have to be driven by a fear of getting hurt. Instead you can develop tools to keep you safe and help you get what you want.

By the way, throughout the book I've avoided repeating expressions like 'he or she' by simply using them pretty much at random. You can relate to either if it's appropriate for you or your partner.

And now, on to your Personal Safety Zone.

What is your Personal Safety Zone?

Your first tool is your Personal Safety Zone.

Personal Safety Zones (PSZs) are about degrees of intimacy. They're there to keep you safe, but they don't work very well if you don't know about them. Everybody has one, so some people tend to assume that everyone else's is the same as theirs. But they aren't.

You probably have a pretty good idea of what you want out of a relationship. Fun; companionship; starry-eyed romance; security; a parent for your child; another notch on the bedpost. But you don't always know the other, more mysterious things you want. The important, secret desires that are really what's driving you. . .and your partner. So let's see what's burrowing away beneath the surface. Then you can take that shadowy, half-formed concept and sharpen it up to be an effective tool in your search for rewarding love.

The most basic question is: how close is too close? How intimate can you be without feeling threatened or invaded? And the next question is: does your Personal Safety Zone match your partner's?

What happens if you don't know about Personal Safety Zones?

You may already be getting an inkling of how this issue has affected your relationships. Let's look at some real-life case histories that show other ways the PSZ plays out.

Cathy's first marriage to a workaholic left her lonely. She wanted real closeness the second time around. Jimmy swept her off her feet with kisses and romance. Within three weeks he moved in – and took over her life. He wouldn't let her out on her own. He spied on her. He embarrassed her by touching her breasts in company. She put up with it for months, swapping her freedom for finally feeling loved. When she did complain he said, 'But I love you! Don't you love me?' What she had thought was love turned out to be a trap. After ten months she sadly threw him out.

Cathy wanted closeness but was afraid of being engulfed. Jimmy was afraid that her need for some space was rejection. When Safety Zones clash, it can be a disaster. Here are some more illustrations of what can happen if your PSZ isn't what you thought it was.

Steve wanted to settle down but was scared of getting close in case he got 'found out' and rejected, so he ended up having soulless one-night stands.

Eleanor, afraid of being hurt, kept choosing partners who couldn't be intimate. Then she'd dump the 'coldhearted rat' and weep – before doing the same thing again.

Marie stayed for fifteen years in a relationship where she was frequently battered. Afraid of being abandoned, she gave her Personal Safety Zone away.

See how these people were tripped up by their Safety Zones? Inside just one person there can be conflicting needs for intimacy and distance, so imagine the permutations when you have two people together!

There are plenty of other uncomfortable ways you can play out this game. Did you recognise any of the ones I've discussed above? Do you have any of your own?

Cathy, Steve and the rest are real people, though naturally I've changed their details to protect their identities. In the book you'll see how they find greater love and fulfilment. The point is, if these people can make the changes they needed in order to get what they want, *so can you*. If what you've been doing so far hasn't worked, why not start filling up your toolkit so your love-life can become rewarding instead of debilitating?

Building your Safe Boundary Framework

To make your PSZ work for you, you'll need to identify what you want in relationships. This is your **Safe Boundary Framework**.

Sadly, if you have conflicting impulses you may not be sure what you really want. You just know you don't want to feel 'like this' any more. That's OK. It's a good starting point. By finding out exactly what you *don't* want, you can move away from it. Then you can target what you *do* want. Bringing your conscious awareness into action gives you a much better chance of getting your needs met!

Start by working out what you don't *want*

The first part of this exercise might be tough, but the second part is more uplifting. You can base it on your own experience and your observation of other people's relationships. There are questions to help you clarify what you want to move away from, with an example of how it works, so you might choose to read on a little before you work out your own answers.

Notice that these questions cover *behaving, feeling* and *thinking* in situations that include you on your own as well as you with your partner. After all, you're half of your relationship and until you're sure of your own needs and desires you limit your chances of getting what you want!

To show how these questions work I've given Cathy's answers. Once you've seen this in action, I'll repeat the questions so you can build your own Safe Boundary Framework.

What won't I be doing
  – with my partner?

I won't be fending him off all the time. I won't be changing my behaviour to fit in with his. I won't have to tell him not to follow me. I won't have to sneak around making calls on my mobile or from a phone box. I won't be hiding how I feel.

  – with my friends and family?

I won't be making excuses or covering up for him. I won't be pushing him away in public. I won't talk about him obsessively with friends to find out what I should do.

  – on my own?

I won't be worrying about what he's up to all the time. I won't be rushing home to avoid another row. I won't wish he was different.

What won't he be doing
  – with me?

He won't grope me in public. He won't follow me everywhere. He won't boss me around. He won't speak for me or smother me. He won't emotionally blackmail me. He won't pressure me sexually when it's inappropriate.

– on his own?

He won't be fretting when I'm not in the same room. He won't phone people to check up on me. He won't mistrust me.

– with other people?

He won't boast about our sex life. He won't touch me up in front of other people. He won't stop me speaking to male friends. He won't lie about me or cause rows to isolate me from other people.

What won't I be feeling?

I won't be feeling trapped, angry, resentful or bitter. I won't be feeling like a naughty, rebellious child. I won't worry all the time what he's doing and saying. I won't feel hounded or smothered. I won't feel powerless.

What won't I be thinking about myself?

I won't be thinking what an idiot I am. I won't be thinking this is the best I can do so there must be something wrong with me. I won't be thinking I'm unkind to push him away when he loves me.

The sorts of things that Cathy came up with may have sparked off some thoughts for you, although you're bound to have ideas of your own.

Here are the questions again, so you can use your own answers to build up your Safe Boundary Framework. Writing your answers down will make your needs clearer and give you more perspective. You may like to have a notebook and pen handy as you work through this and the following exercises.

What won't I be doing
– with my partner?
– with my friends and family?
– on my own?

What won't she be doing
— with me?
— on her own?
— with other people?

What won't I be feeling?

What won't I be thinking about myself?

Work out what you want instead

Now you can have fun with the positive part. You start by building a fantasy picture of your ideal relationship. The more details you can come up with in each of the three aspects – *behaving, feeling* and *thinking* – the better. All three areas are vital because they help you clarify the boundaries of what feels safe for you. Once you've got your dream the way you want it, you can use the questions below to study it and find out what level of intimacy you're actually looking for. Again, I invite you to look at Cathy's answers first. Your answers will almost certainly be different, but seeing how someone else sets up their Safe Boundary Framework shows this tool in operation.

This is what Cathy put:

What do I want?

I want a man who will respect my privacy; who will let me be myself and love me as I am. I want us both to have our own space as well as some shared space.

What will I be doing
— with my partner?

I'll be able to get on with my life in peace. I'll be able to ask him for help when I need it. I'll talk easily with him but feel comfortable in the silences. I'll share some activities with him but not all. I'll be myself. I'll be an equal partner.

– with my friends and family?

I'll talk to them about him but about other things as well. I'll spend time with them whether he's there or not.

– on my own?

I can have a bath, relax or do chores in peace. I'll go out on my own sometimes.

What will he be doing
– with me?

He'll be comfortable with me whether we're talking or not. He'll kiss me hello and goodbye, and sometimes snuggle with me on the sofa. He'll let me make the first move in sex sometimes. He'll go out with me to places I like sometimes, and he'll hold my hand in public when it's appropriate. He'll listen to me seriously and negotiate. He'll be supportive.

– on his own?

He'll be able to entertain himself and act responsibly. He'll be independent.

– with other people?

He'll have his own friends. He'll introduce me to his friends and family. He'll accept my right to be with my friends and family. He'll talk to them amicably. He'll be affectionate in a socially acceptable way.

What will I be feeling?

I'll be feeling safe, wanted and secure. I'll trust him and feel trusted. I'll feel proud of him. I'll feel confident and relaxed. I'll feel we belong together. I'll feel happy when I think of him. I'll feel cherished and valued.

What will I be thinking about myself?

I'll be thinking I made the right decision and I deserve someone this good.

Now you've seen how Cathy worked out what level of closeness she felt comfortable with. But of course you have your own individual needs and desires around intimacy.

You are allowed to feel what you feel and know what you want. Please remember that *what you want is as important as what anybody else wants*. It doesn't matter whether that's a partner, your mother or some authority figure. What you're doing here isn't against any law. It's working out what feels good and safe for you. In this process you may be tempted into *should* and *ought* territory, as though somehow you didn't feel right putting any importance on your own views. There'll be more about this later. For now it's enough to know that so long as you don't want to hurt anyone deliberately and against their will, you can discover what's right for you. That will form your Safe Boundary Framework so that relationships work better for you. Isn't that what you want?

I invite you now to work out your own answers to these questions about doing, thinking and feeling:

What do I want?

What will I be doing
  – with my partner?
  – with my friends and family?
  – on my own?

What will she be doing
  – with me?
  – on her own?
  – with other people?

What will I be feeling?

What will I be thinking about myself?

Summary
Your Personal Safety Zone is about how much intimacy and how much space you want. The first step in making your PSZ work for you is building your Safe Boundary Framework by having clear guidelines of what you do and don't want so that love feels good for you.

2

—

The 'Old Rules' Eraser

If your old relationship rules kept getting you hurt,
you can replace them with supportive permissions

What rules do you play by?
Now you've got your Safe Boundary Framework, you can make
your Personal Safety Zone more effective by updating your beliefs
about how relationships work.

Most people have a set of unwritten 'rules' that they operate by
in relationships. You soak these old rules up from everything
around you: school, soap operas, love songs and so on, but especially your home.

That means every single person has their own set of unwritten
rules. They're almost certainly different from your partner's, but
your rules and his will probably feel like they match up to bind
you together – or keep you apart. You may think some are true for
you but not for others.

The one common thread is: *how much are you prepared to put
up with?*

Some people are willing to put up with anything to keep their
partner. How often have you heard – or said – 'But I can't leave
him! I love him!' I invite you to read through the list of old rules
below and see if any of these have helped keep you stuck.

Old relationship rules

1. *You're no good without a partner.*
2. *True love never runs smooth.*
3. *Any partner is better than none.*
4. *You're not good enough so you'll never get what you want.*
5. *You have to do what your partner wants, however painful.*
6. *Your partner's feelings are more important than yours.*
7. *You're not allowed to have power in relationships (except by dumping someone).*
8. *You have to stay loyal regardless.*
9. *You have to accept what your partner says even if it means ignoring what she does.*
10. *You have to pretend the bad things didn't happen or didn't matter.*
11. *You have to try really hard to please your partner if you're going to get any attention – which you probably won't.*
12. *You can 'fix' this person's problems so they'll be grateful and repay you by staying.*
13. *You'll never find another one like him.*
14. *Without this partner you'll always be alone and unloved.*

What do old relationship rules get you?

Let's see what effect these old rules had on one of my clients.

Hughie, a good man with a steady job in a big firm, married flirty Anita from the wages office. Everybody but Hughie knew she kept having affairs. The signs were there – lies and evasions, coldness, 'harmless' flirtations under his nose, silent phone calls and mysterious, expensive presents. To him, love had always felt full of pain and insecurity. If he said anything she made him feel guilty and disloyal for his doubts. He went to pieces when she finally left him for another man. He hadn't seen it coming because he'd played by his old rules.

It's easy to see when it's laid out for you, but much harder when it's your life and you're living it one day at a time. Hughie's despair led him to update his hurtful old rules. He's happy now with a loving partner and two gorgeous kids.

I invite you to take a minute and read each of the old rules again. Ask yourself two questions: have you ever operated by any of them? And here's the killer. If you have kept these old rules, *did they get you what you really want?*

Why do people keep these old rules?

If you recognise any of these old rules, it probably reflects what's been going on for you at least some of the time. They probably felt normal to you. That's because:

- People unconsciously pick partners whose 'ruled' behaviour fits their own, so they have a ready-made way of relating to people who have a ready-made way of relating to them.

- It does get some of your needs met some of the time – though at a cost.

- It lets you feel that you're the good guy.

- Conversely, it may confirm your old belief that there's something wrong with you and you deserve to suffer.

- Each time you go down the same route, it 'proves' to you that that's how things are and always will be.

- Played at a low to moderate level, it gives you something to talk about. Women get together and enjoy a good old moan about men. Men exclaim, 'Women!' It makes you members of the same club.

Breaking the rules

Keeping those old rules doesn't work. So can you change?

Let's split that question into three parts. Does the whole world play by exactly the same old rules as you? No.

Can people who used to follow these old rules change? Yes. Thousands of people have realised their old rules didn't work so, like Hughie, they've updated them and they're happier.

Finally, can you, personally, change? Yes. Definitely. *If you choose to.*

Once you realise the old rules didn't get you what you really wanted, you can start to see the possibility of different, more comfortable ways to relate. If other people can do it, so can you, especially as you develop supportive beliefs to help you.

Are you willing to say right now, 'I give myself permission to do things differently from here on in'?

If you are, congratulations! Take a moment to feel good about that.

But once you've chucked out the old rules that made up your relationship route-map, there's a big hole where they used to be. What can you replace them with? The **'Old Rules' Eraser** will show you.

The 'Old Rules' Eraser

Here's where you get what may be some of the most important sentences in the English language. They are called permissions.

Each of these permissions replaces one or more of those bad old you-know-whats. It helps to say each permission out loud over and over every day until they drown out the old rules. You can also write them down and carry them around to look at frequently.

1. *I'm allowed to exist as my own, valuable person whether I'm with someone or not.*

2. *I'm OK as I am. Even if I'm not particularly thrilled with how I am right now, I'm still growing and evolving so it's OK to be me where I am on my journey through life.*

3. *I'm good enough for me so I'm good enough for you.*

4. *I'm allowed to feel my feelings and trust them to tell me what's really going on.*

5. *I'm allowed to know what I know and think what I think.*

6. *I'm allowed not to trust people until they've earned my trust by what they do.*

7. *I'm allowed to be as important as everybody else.*

8. *I'm allowed to be good at relationships now, and I can learn what I need in order to do this.*

9. *I'm allowed to have fun and feel good about myself.*

10. *I'm allowed to be as grown up and independent as I want to be. I'm responsible for myself and nobody else (unless I have kids or other dependants).*

11. *I'm allowed to be as close to people as I want to be.*

12. *If it doesn't feel good at least 90 per cent of the time, it isn't love.*

13. *Men/women really are like buses. There's always another one behind.*

Notice this last one. In the past you may have subscribed to the notion that there's only one true love of your life, whether you've met them yet or not. This is not true, and it's responsible for more misery than I can say. People don't go round with big signs over their heads saying, 'The love of Jessica's life' or 'The only girl for Michael'. My husband and I are extremely happy together but if

I die first, I'd like to think that he'll go on to find happiness with someone else.

Also, just because you think you love someone, you don't have to cling on for grim death if the relationship doesn't turn out to be such a good idea (though it takes some of us a long time to find this out!) Sure, there'll be *aspects* of people that you love and *aspects* of you that they love, but it doesn't mean that's the only relationship you're ever allowed to have. People move on and that's OK. Splitting up doesn't mean there's anything wrong with either of you. You are allowed to check people out and decide whether to stay. Or not.

By using these permissions to erase your old rules, you'll start feeling more positive about yourself so you'll begin to enjoy a growing sensation of your personal power.

Soon you'll have plenty of chances to try out your new ways of behaving, thinking and feeling. After all, there are plenty more pebbles on the beach!

Summary
Erasing your old relationship rules with a set of positive permissions allows you to feel happier and more in control. You *can* do something different with partners from now on.

3

—

The Sabotage Squelch

Have you unknowingly been making it harder to have good relationships? Now you can recognise self-sabotage and replace it with confidence and hope

Using your Personal Safety Zone

You've got a clearer idea of what you want and you're starting to change your beliefs about how relationships work. I hope you're beginning to feel less like a victim of fate or chance and more like you're gaining control. Now it's time to find out what you need to do to *use* your Personal Safety Zone.

Because your PSZ tells you how safe you feel with the amount of intimacy you're experiencing, it lets you know when it's time to act. But if you don't think you can get what you want, you might ignore its promptings. In other words, self-doubt can sabotage you, so it's time to replace it with confidence and hope. This might be a challenge, but wouldn't it be worth the effort if you could put yourself in the driver's seat of your life?

How do self-sabotaging beliefs work?

Earlier you saw how Jimmy thought Cathy's need for space was a rejection of him. Cathy, ignoring the promptings of her PSZ, put up with his invasiveness because she wanted love at any price. It wasn't helpful – but they were both acting out their underlying beliefs. Jimmy subconsciously believed he'd be abandoned. By controlling Cathy he *tried* to achieve a deep and lasting attachment – but what he *got* was the rejection he was focused on.

With a broken marriage behind her, Cathy believed she wasn't lovable. She *tried* to be Jimmy's perfect girlfriend so she wouldn't end up alone – but how did she end up? Alone. Even though she thought she was acting to safeguard her future, her beliefs sabotaged her attempt to find love.

Although nobody sabotages themselves consciously, your hidden belief system affects everything you do. Whether it's a question of shyness so you don't get started, or picking the wrong people, or just not getting on as well as you'd like with your partner, there's a good chance your belief system needs a tune-up. And what wonderful results await you!

Why do we have self-sabotaging beliefs?

It's amazing how you get what you're focused on. People go along quite happily thinking their beliefs will protect them. But they don't.

That's what those old, self-sabotaging beliefs were designed for: protection. Maybe they haven't worked out for you as well as you'd hoped but you don't need to start beating yourself up. Your old beliefs have got you through this far. You're still alive and still more or less intact, so they worked to some extent. Think of them as a rough sketch that you're now turning into a beautiful painting.

These beliefs formed part of your identity ('I'm too shy to get what I want,' for example), but they limited your notions about what you could do. When you were growing up, such beliefs helped you fit in with the people around you – especially adults, who were powerful when you were small and dependent. You formulated your beliefs the best way you could with the resources that were available to you as a child. But now you're an adult and you're allowed to have helpful adult beliefs.

It's always easier to spot other people's blind spots than your own. That's why they're called blind spots! Your belief system has probably been there almost as long as you have. Because you've always believed it, you've never questioned it. In every crack in relationships, most people automatically look for the 'evidence' that lets them go. 'See? I was right! I am a failure/unlovable/ doomed to be alone.' My own past belief that I wasn't allowed to belong came partly from not having the same accent as the other kids at school, so I got picked on. Later, because I didn't believe I could belong, I unconsciously picked people who wouldn't *let* me belong! Each unhappy relationship seemed to 'prove' I didn't belong. I kept doing the same things over and over – and getting the same painful results. Challenging my old beliefs was hard, but it's transformed my life in the most rewarding ways!

Typically, sabotaging beliefs are things like: 'There's something wrong with me', 'Nobody will ever love me' or 'I'll never get what I want'. And remember, they are *old* beliefs. Archaic. You can change them and form new beliefs. After all, you had the power to form the old ones when you were just a kid – a time when you also may have believed monsters lurked under your bed. Now it's time for some grown-up beliefs.

And think how much more you can do now you're an adult! You can thank those old beliefs for doing their best to protect you – and *you can make new beliefs that are more helpful.* Because an updated, supportive belief system is the next tool you need to make your Personal Safety Zone work for you.

The Sabotage Squelch

Do you want to find out if you've been maintaining beliefs that have kept you stuck up to now? The goal is to identify that old pre-programming and update it – a tool I've called the **Sabotage Squelch**. Once you believe it's possible for you to get what you want, you won't have to put up with second best, and you'll have more choice in how you behave in relationships.

What you do is take two pieces of paper. On the first you put the heading 'Old Beliefs'. By the way, you may feel that looking at them closely seems pretty scary – but don't worry. Like most 'monsters', once you get them out into the light of day, they're nowhere near as frightening as you thought. Especially as you're going to update them with new and positive beliefs that will work not *against* you, but *for* you. The second piece of paper will be for your 'Positive Supporting Beliefs'.

Once again, you can see how this worked for someone else before you fill yours in. **Jenny**'s answers are fairly typical of the ones I hear in counselling because lots of people start out with this sort of belief system. I know I did! If you believe anything like this, you're not alone, and like Jenny and me and thousands of others, you can change *if you're willing to*.

Jenny was sweet, pretty, single and in her thirties. None of her relationships had lasted long and some had been abusive. When she came to therapy she was lonely and sad. She'd always felt like an outsider and wanted things to be different. And they are, now that she's changed her beliefs! She's happy and popular and delighted to be in love with a good, caring man. First, though, she had to do some work.

These are the outdated, self-sabotaging beliefs Jenny found and changed:

Old beliefs

    – Can I have good relationships?

No.

– What 'evidence' do I have?

I always end up alone, the odd one out. Richard and David dumped me. Jamie two-timed me and Alec lied. My friends are married but I'm not.

– Have I ever had a good relationship of any sort?

No. I've always felt unloved and criticised by my mother. My father abandoned us when I was six years old. My best friend betrayed with me. My teachers ignored me. I can't join in with anyone.

– How do other people really feel about me?

They don't like me. They'll never accept me. They're all right and I'm not. They're allowed to belong and I'm not.

– What do people see when they look at me?

Someone pale and nervous who can't speak up for herself or join in.

– What do I think about myself when relationships go wrong?

Typical. I'll always be rejected. There must be something wrong with me. I'm not like other people. I don't belong and I'll never get what I want.

– What's my worst nightmare?

I'll die a sad, bitter, lonely old woman.

– How do I feel about that emotionally and physically?

Lonely, frightened, full of dread for the future. I can't stop thinking about it. It keeps me awake or I have nightmares that leave my heart pounding.

– What emotions wasn't I allowed to show as a child?

I was punished for showing anger, sadness and fear.

Poor Jenny! No wonder her past relationships had brought her nothing but sadness. Her 'evidence' supported her old beliefs, and her old beliefs kept her clinging desperately to relationships that were doomed to end in pain. She didn't think she was allowed to use her feelings to protect herself. Can you see how she was unconsciously sabotaging herself?

As you now answer the same questions for yourself, please remember that these are *old* beliefs that you developed when you were a young, vulnerable child. You can feel compassion for the child who lived with those painful beliefs. Now you've grown up, and you can think more clearly. Identifying what you want to change helps you build the supportive beliefs you need, so even if the first part of this exercise feels depressing, you can congratulate yourself on being brave enough to bring the 'monster' into the light. And you've got the uplifting part to look forward to. So why not fill in the old beliefs that you're about to change?

Your old beliefs

Can I have good relationships?
What 'evidence' do I have?
Have I ever had a good relationship of any sort?
How do other people really feel about me?
What do people see when they look at me?
What do I think about myself when relationships go wrong?
What's my worst nightmare?
How do I feel about all this?
What emotions wasn't I allowed to show as a child?

Building positive supporting beliefs

Well done! Squelching your self-sabotaging beliefs may have been tough, but here comes the good part. Now you've discovered what it is that you want to be different, you can replace those old ideas with positive supporting beliefs. By the way, it can be very satisfying to burn or tear up the 'Old Beliefs' sheet before you go any further!

When you come to fill in your 'Positive Supporting Beliefs' sheet, you look for *positive* evidence with every single question. Any of it, however small. A smile, a single act of kindness, a compliment you once received. Evidence that you've been accepted, liked, loved, listened to or valued, even for a moment. Evidence of good feelings, however brief. Because if good things happened once, they can happen again. Just being able to change 'never' or 'always' to 'sometimes' is a step in the right direction.

Again, before you answer the questions for yourself, here are Jenny's responses to spark off your own ideas. If she *hadn't* been able to come up with anything positive, a good fantasy would be a challenge to her old beliefs just by itself. And the same goes for you. Good luck!

Positive supporting beliefs

Can I have good relationships?

Yes.

What evidence do I have?

Part of the time I felt safe and wanted with Richard, David and Alec. I had a good laugh with Jamie. Andrew said I was good company. Lou cuddled me a lot.

Have I ever had a good relationship of any sort?

Some of the time, as above. My mother did her best for me

even if it didn't always feel that good, but I'm glad she valued me enough to make the effort. One of my lecturers was kind. My boss says I get on well with my customers and I have a laugh with them. Nadine chats to me. My cousin and her kids love me. I feel relaxed with them. I can sometimes join in the conversation in the canteen and I get asked to parties.

How do other people feel about me?

Some people like me. Richard, Alec and Jamie wanted to be closer to me. My lecturer and my boss helped me when I asked. Other people aren't always happy so I'm the same. My cousin and her kids love me. Mum loves me in her own way. Other people's relationships go wrong too – like Mum's! Her and Dad's problems weren't my fault.

What do people see when they look at me?

A good listener. My boss and my customers see someone friendly who does a good job. Richard, Alec and Jamie saw someone they wanted to be closer to. My mother saw someone worth struggling to provide for. Jamie saw someone who is a laugh. Andrew saw me as good company. Lou saw me as cuddly. Nadine says I'm smart and sympathetic.

What do I think about myself?

It's not just me – sometimes other people are unhappy too. So I'm like them. I'm acceptable and valuable. I might not be perfect but nobody else is either. And I'm getting to be more how I want every day. I'm likable. I can be close to friends and colleagues. I'm popular with my customers. I'm smart and sympathetic. I've had lots of boyfriends so I know I can attract men. I'm a good laugh. I'm cuddly. I'm easy to talk to and a good listener. I'm helpful. I can be comfortable with workmates, customers, my cousin's lot and other people. I can have fun and belong with people. I'm lovable.

What's my most cherished fantasy?

I'll be a happy, fulfilled wife and mother with lots of friends.

How do I feel about all this?

I feel good. I like having hope. I like knowing I'm in the same boat as other people. I can like myself for my good qualities (now I know I have some!) I feel more relaxed. I'm glad my busy mother did the best she could for me because I'm worth it. I'm pleased I'm popular with my customers and and that I have some good friends. I'm loved and accepted by my cousin and her kids and I'm glad I'm lovable. I can relax with other people, talk easily, share jokes and have fun.

What emotions am I allowed to show now?

I can show all my emotions. I can trust them to guide me and protect me. I can use my anger to defend myself, and my sadness and fear to know what I want to move away from. I'm allowed to be happy.

This worked like a charm for Jenny, and many others. Are you ready to build your own positive supportiving beliefs? Here are the questions as a guide.

Your positive supporting beliefs
Can I have good relationships?
What 'evidence' do I have?
Have I ever had a good relationship of any sort?
How do I think other people really feel about me?
What do people see when they look at me?
What do I think about myself now?

What's my most cherished fantasy?
How do I feel about all this?
What emotions am I allowed to show now?

I hope you've found, in fantasy or memory, many examples of good things that have happened for you, and that you're now starting to enjoy a more positive view of yourself – even if it's only in one or two small areas at first. The more positives you can think of, the faster you'll squelch those old self-sabotaging beliefs.

Reinforcing your positive self-image

As you concentrate on positive memories, you will start to feel more confident. You can reinforce your self-esteem further by deliberately investing time and energy in positive fantasies.

Cathy, for example, had for years harboured a narrow, freeze-frame image of herself as a lonely old woman with only the TV for company. Now I encouraged her to widen that image and add positives to it. She pictured the door to her room and imagined a nice old gentleman coming in with two mugs of cocoa. As she began to believe she was lovable and wouldn't end up abandoned, she felt much less self-conscious. She was able to build herself a social life and be more picky about partners. Since few people want to end up alone, she found a lot more choice than she'd thought was out there!

Other examples of transforming negative images into support-ive ones include:

- The woman who changed her picture of her lonely deathbed into a sun-lounger by the sparkling Mediterranean, with a partner bringing her a cocktail from a beach-bar. She found the courage to start dating again.

- The shy man who dwelt on nightmares of people laughing at him. He consciously went back in his fantasy to a few moments before, when he'd told a brilliant joke. He now had the confidence to talk to people.

- Steve, who kept dreaming he was trapped alone in shadows behind a high wall while everyone else was outside having a ball in the sunshine. Dreams have their own symbolic logic, so he consciously imagined he grew wings and flew over to join the party. Once he'd done this he found in real life that he could talk to girls, not just flirt with them.

- The woman who viewed herself trudging alone down an endless grey tunnel. She transformed its grey walls into mist so she could walk out into a bright, lively village fete where she joined in at the stalls and had a laugh with other holiday-makers. The real-life effect was that she stopped going out with any passing guy who asked her, and now that she'd stopped feeling desperate, she began to attract men who'd be better partners for her.

Each of these people found positive fantasies revitalising. They now felt much more optimistic and could act with more confidence. After all, optimism is a much more attractive trait than hopelessness! It's also much nicer as a way of life – and you can start building it now.

Positive fantasies are a great investment. They'll reinforce your good feelings about yourself and give you hope for the future. They work especially well if, from now on, you look at every single smile or chat or act of kindness as a reminder of your worth. Would you rather stay stuck or will you give optimism a shot? You have nothing but unhelpful old beliefs to lose and only positive benefits to gain!

Summary

Old childhood beliefs can sabotage you because they affect the way you behave, but now you can squelch them with supportive beliefs that help you get more of what you want. You can build confidence and hope by investing time in positive fantasies. Now you can let your Personal Safety Zone work for you!

Clearing Your Past History

Has your old relationship style been hurtful? Here's how you can start changing your old ways of being with partners, and build nourishing relationships instead

The **Pattern Transformation** helps you identify common painful elements in your past relationships and start changing them.

When partners haven't turned out as you expected, the **Fantasy Filter** shows you how to recognise projections and respond to reality.

Have you ever kicked yourself for letting others manipulate you? The **Powerhouse** helps you stop being used and start getting more of the attention you want.

When you've felt powerless in relationships, the **Reality Key** lets you increase your personal effectiveness.

If you've ever felt broken-hearted, your **First Aid Kit** helps you let go of pain and create a brighter future.

4

—

The Pattern Transformation

Have there been common painful elements in your past relationships? This tool shows you how to start putting an end to old patterns and relationship games

Why look for common elements in past relationships?

People who've been hurt in love often bring two painful thoughts to counselling: 'I'm back to square one' and 'I've got to put the past behind me.' Mostly they don't see the contradiction between these two statements. Of course they don't always use these words precisely, but I often hear people expressing their reluctance to 'rake it all up again'. Do you have your own version of this?

I agree that it isn't pleasant to relive the pain, but if you keep behaving in exactly the same ways, you'll keep getting exactly the same results. Wouldn't it make sense to find out how you got hurt and do something different to make your love-life more rewarding?

How do you spend your time with your partner?

For now let's ignore children, relatives and friends and concentrate on how you and your partner spend your time together.

Here's a short quiz. There are two columns, one for your answers and one for your partner's. If you're not with someone right now you can pick up the pattern from your last relationship. The choices for your answers are 'Never', 'Sometimes', and 'Often'. Because this is about your responses, you also get to put the answer for the other person the way you see it.

	What I do	What s/he does
Choose to spend more time apart than together		
When together, scarcely look at partner		
When together, scarcely talk to partner		
Stick to neutral subjects		
Avoid expressing feelings		
In arguments, try to hurt or score points		
Try to get attention by pleasing partner		
Nurture partner		
Feel nurtured by partner		
Scarcely touch partner		
Only touch for sex		
Only have sex when other person wants		

	What I do	**What s/he does**
Divide chores fairly		
Share leisure activities		
Enjoy own separate leisure activities		

There are no right or wrong answers and no marks for what you put. Instead you're examining *your* feelings about what's going on for you. For each question, if you feel that you and any partner have the balance right, you can sketch a smiley face at the end of the line. If you feel more or less OK about an answer, put a face with a straight line for a mouth, and if you're unhappy, sketch a face with a downturned mouth.

What this part of the exercise highlights is how happy you are with the ways you and your partners spend time together.

Remember, right now we're talking about *your* feelings, not your partner's. Later in the book you'll find ways of recognising partners you're likely to be happy with and negotiating for more of what you want. For the moment, you're on a fact-finding mission and checking out your own responses. This and the following chapters show you how to use this knowledge to build positive strategies for getting what you want.

Have you transferred your pattern of spending time together?

Now think back to earlier relationships. Though there may be some differences between present and previous partnerships, people are often amazed to find that the way they've structured time in each relationship is pretty much the same. In other words, they've *transferred the pattern* of behaviours that let them get close to – or stay distanced from – their partner. If you now answer the same questions for you and past partners, how true is this for you?

You may be wondering why this is, and if you're not comfortable with your pattern, how to do something different.

Let's start with the *why* part. Every man, woman and child on this planet was born with the need to be acknowledged. Babies cry for attention because without it they'd die. Adults may be able to fend for themselves but the need for recognition is still there. People learn how to get attention (or avoid it) in their family of origin, where their survival depended on it. They don't always realise that now they're independent they can update their patterns of behaviour to get the attention they want while keeping themselves safe in adult ways. Loneliness is an unpleasant but widespread feeling – and it's based on that inborn need to be acknowledged.

However, we don't always feel safe asking directly for attention. In Western society people are commonly taught that it's either 'big-headed' or 'whingeing' to call attention to yourself. In some cultures there's a phenomenon called 'tall poppy syndrome', which means that if you stand out you'll be punished in some way, just as a poppy that stands above the others could get its head lopped off.

But everybody needs recognition. Sometimes they get it by manipulation or emotional blackmail. And sometimes they just fall for the first person who pays them any attention at all. That's often the case with whirlwind romances, which is one reason for the saying 'Marry in haste, repent at leisure.' After the novelty of a new relationship has worn off, most people stop being on their best behaviour and unconsciously go back to their underlying pattern of organising their time with others (the pattern they learned in childhood). If that's the case in your life, you could be feeling ignored and undervalued. Unless, of course, you've found new behaviours that let you get enough contact and still feel safe.

Has this been true for you? If so, could you usefully update your pattern transfer?

Pattern transfers are about how you make contact

In order to transform your old patterns to more rewarding ones, you can use your emotional responses. The smiling, neutral and sad faces you drew for your answers are your clues.

It's important to remember that *you* experience life through *your* senses. Yours are the eyes you see through, the body that lets you know what feels comfortable, the ears that hear whether things sound good, and the mind that makes sense of what goes on. It's all very noble making excuses for the other person ('Her work is demanding' or 'He's been hurt so I have to be forgiving') but at the end of the day, if what's going on doesn't feel good to you, it's *not* good for you and that's that. I appreciate that in special circumstances it may be necessary to put up with things you don't like *for a while*, but if this goes on for a long time or is a repeating pattern, isn't it worth questioning whether different ways of being with a partner could be more rewarding?

So what are the choices in the way people organise their time? In other words, what is the *pattern of getting attention (or not getting it) that you want to transform?*

First, there's *emotional absence*. This means withdrawing. You can do this in the same room as someone else, perhaps by watching TV or reading. By not making contact, you're not risking rejection. Sometimes it's nice to chill out quietly with someone, but if you feel alone and cut off, that's emotional absence.

Next comes *recognition*. For example, saying 'Hi!' is recognition. If someone you know has passed you in the street without at least a wave you may have felt slightly hurt, which is one way of noticing that recognition matters. Or you and your partner may just exchange a brief hello in passing. Neither of you has taken the time to establish any intimacy here. You haven't risked much in the way of rejection.

Impersonal contact is the next stage. You might talk about neutral subjects like the weather, engines, kids today or anything which isn't personal. It's cocktail party talk, merely superficial. Nothing is solved. Nothing gets done (although you do get a chance to start sussing out the other person and it can be an entertaining way of passing the time). But if someone turned down your conversational overture you might feel somewhat rejected.

Parallel contact implies a contradiction. You and the other person are engaged in a task together. It could be work. It could be a shared hobby. You are achieving something together and it can be companionable. But you are not revealing yourself and nor is the other person, so there's no real emotional contact. Parallel lines, of course, never touch.

With *manipulative contact* you open yourself up a little more, but indirectly. This might be where you clean your boyfriend's flat or fix your girlfriend's car in order to get some attention – and it doesn't work. You feel let down or hurt; the other person is mystified that you're upset; and both of you end up feeling puzzled and uncomfortable. You both recognise that you've been through this before but don't really understand how you've got there. Manipulative contact has got you some fairly potent attention but neither of you feel good.

Intimate contact is where you and the other person share how you're really feeling. This may be pleasant: genuine lovemaking, an expression of caring, a shared glance of amusement. Telling the other person you're hurt, angry, scared or sad are also authentic expressions of how you feel. Good or painful, intimate contact means you've invited the other person to recognise the real, emotional you and so it carries the highest risk of rejection as well as the biggest potential rewards.

So how do you feel now about your pattern transfer? Do you

want to make it more satisfying – by switching to **Pattern Transformation?**

The Pattern Transformation

Finding out how you've been transferring your pattern of seeking attention is the first part of the solution. It lets you know there are other options. How to find those options and feel comfortable carrying them out is the subject of the next few chapters. For now, here are some practical tips.

- The beginning of a relationship shows you how you and your partner use your time to make or avoid contact. Look at what's going on between you. If you're doing all the running, that's probably how it will stay. If that's not what you want, you can either ask outright for what you want or find someone else who automatically gives you enough attention.

- People have to earn trust. If someone does what they say when they say they will, you can begin to trust them. If they let you down, or are very late more than three times, it may be worth rethinking your relationship plans. If the person isn't honest, reliable and open, is that trustworthy? Do you want to be excluded and kept in the dark?

- If the person only touches you for sexual purposes, that is not an expression of valuing you.

- If you and the other person can't talk together in a relaxed and comfortable way by the third or fourth date, you probably never will.

- If after four to six weeks you still feel you have to be on your best behaviour, this relationship may not be the one for you.

You may also need to build up your self-esteem so you don't feel dependent on other people's acceptance. The 'You and Your Needs' section at the beginning of this book will help greatly with this, and there are other resources listed at the back of the book. Your local library may have information on local confidence and assertiveness courses.

Summary
The pattern transfer is the set of behaviours you carry from one relationship to the next to get attention. You can start transforming it to something more comfortable by realising that repeating old, unhelpful patterns will get you the same unhelpful results. The following chapters show you how to transform your pattern in more detail.

5

The Fantasy Filter

When partners haven't turned out as you expected, the Fantasy Filter shows you how to recognise projections and respond to reality

How we make contact

In the last chapter you learned about the different levels of making (or avoiding) contact. Although mood and events can affect this, other factors can too.

Just think of the range of ways of dealing with one particular situation – for example, coming home after a bad day. Some people want peace and quiet to recover, others silently curse themselves and the world or blot out everything with drink (emotional absence). They may have a good moan, rage blamefully, take out their anger by making someone else feel bad (impersonal or manipulative contact), or ask openly for support (intimacy).

We all use some of these sometimes, but which of these pattern transfer options do you use most often? Which ones have your partners used with you? Do you think this could also be because of how you see yourself and your partner?

Projections

Few people would knowingly go into a relationship with a bully, an emotional blackmailer or someone who will neglect them – unless they believe they have no other option. But if people see themselves as powerless to escape from loneliness, they might accept any contact at all as being better than none. This is the same for the bullies, the blackmailers and those who neglect their partners.

And what about you? Just knowing that someone sometimes acknowledges you can feel better than being alone, at least for a while. If you don't feel very good about yourself, you might find that being alone gives you plenty of time to listen to painful, self-critical thoughts. Then you might hope that having a partner, even a neglectful or abusive one, will give you some recognition, some status that will temporarily allow you to think better of yourself.

However, people don't always see themselves as they really are, let alone see how other people are. This is what lies beneath the pattern transfer. Influenced by unconscious memories of a time when you were small and helpless and adults were big and powerful, you may believe that you don't have what it takes to get the attention you'd like. If you haven't updated those old beliefs you might mistakenly think others are more valuable or more important than you, so you might not feel safe asking for the contact you need.

If you see others as more powerful than you, what they do – or don't do – takes on a significance out of all proportion to reality. If your boyfriend doesn't ring when he said he would, you might feel completely devastated and utterly worthless. If the woman you fancy talks to you, you might feel you're walking on air. In other words, you are projecting an image of your partner as some superhuman being who can make everything wonderful or awful, while the image you see of yourself is negligible. Projections are the unrealistic images you might have of yourself or others. When you're stressed, you may well find yourself responding to these projections rather than reality.

One way of describing these projections is as masks. Have you ever felt the need to hide behind a mask? Or have you ever fallen for someone you thought was great, but who then really let you down?

Fantasy roles in relationships

People with a poor self-image mistakenly discount their good qualities. On their mental screen they project a negative image of themselves. We can call these Frog Prince or Cinderella masks.

When self-doubting people begin a relationship, the positive attention they receive may temporarily cover over their under-lying self-critical Cinderella or Frog Prince mask with a more upbeat Hero or Angel mask. Particularly if both partners are coming from some feeling of desperation, the upbeat masks oper-ate powerfully. Each partner *believes* they love the other because of the temporary relief their own upbeat masks offer. That's why people say love is blind.

As you can see, both partners have a lot invested in maintain-ing their own positive mask and that of the other person. Sometimes this means glossing over or excusing poor treatment. Sometimes it means taking all the blame, perhaps by mistakenly believing that they deserve neglect or abuse or that they had the power to provoke their partner into behaving badly. But when the Hero or Angel masks inevitably slip, the sudden plunge into despair leads both parties to demonise the other person. This works both ways, but here is a typical scenario.

Louise, a thirty-something businesswoman, came to coun-selling after two painful relationships, when **Roy,** her third boyfriend, suddenly broke off all contact without a word of expla-nation. They had been going out together for five years. Roy had often promised marriage but it had never happened. And now he'd abandoned her. He wouldn't answer her phone calls or even open his door to her. Only her responsibility for her nine-year-old son kept Louise from taking an overdose, although she realised this was an unfair burden on a child.

Gradually, in counselling, Louise realised that her relationship with Roy had never been good. At the start he'd declared undying devotion, saying that she had rescued him from the pits of despair. Once she was going out with him he no longer had the panic attacks which had started when his wife had divorced him. He called Louise his 'angel', and though at heart Louise felt deeply unworthy, she tried to live up to the mask of Angel which he had projected onto her. Later, when Roy offered little attention, Louise worked even harder at being Angelic to manipulate him into making contact. Part of the Angel mask was that Louise didn't say a word Roy didn't want to hear.

Roy's attentions, however sporadic, allowed her to keep that Angel mask between her and her Cinderella insecurities so that when he was nice to her she felt good. This caused her to see Roy as her Hero because – at times – he saved her from pain. He valued his Hero mask because it offered some protection from his own underlying existential despair, but when the Hero mask slipped and he saw himself as the worthless Frog Prince, his guilt and Louise's criticisms made him withdraw into drink to avoid the pain of the rejection he expected. Each of them plunged from the fantasy world of Hero and Angel into the self-loathing of their negative projections, and now felt that the other was some malevolent demon with infinite power to hurt.

Why get rid of the fantasy?

It is these fantasy masks, particularly the inner, self-condemnatory beliefs, which keep unrewarding relationships going. To maintain the fantasy, people are prepared to put up with emotional absence, manipulative contact or abuse – in fact, anything to avoid true intimacy, which each partner fears because they believe that would mean showing their unworthy inner mask.

However it is only when *all* the masks are stripped away that change becomes possible. That means getting rid of the distorted Hero and Angel disguises as well as the mistaken Cinderella/Frog Prince masks underneath.

Nobody deserves bad relationships. Just because bad things have happened to you in the past it doesn't mean you can't have good things in the future. You can. Shame and guilt are very powerful forces – but they are not truths, they are *perceptions*. Masks. So is the view that others have the power of life and death over you. The **Fantasy Filter** is a tool to get rid of the masks.

The Fantasy Filter

So how can you filter out these fantasy projections? Take off your own and your partner's masks? I invite you to read through the exercise, then see how Louise made it work before you come back and do it for yourself.

Step 1: Think of a time in your most recent relationship when you felt bad. Ask yourself whether you've felt this way before. Does this uncomfortable feeling (of helplessness, worthlessness, invisibility or whatever) come up for you often? Does it remind you of anything or anyone in your childhood? Can you name that feeling?

Step 2: Close your eyes and take a couple of slow, deep breaths. Imagine you can see yourself as a child with that uncomfortable feeling. (If you can't remember your childhood, imagine what it would be like for another boy or girl.) Quite often it helps if you can mentally look down and see what shoes you were wearing. From there you can often work out where you were and who was with you – in other words, who was discounting the real you. The you now, with your adult resources, can be an invisible presence viewing the past scene.

Step 3: Imagine the invisible adult you has a magic pause button. Watch the younger you and when she acts (or doesn't act) because of that inner, painful belief, imagine your invisible adult self pressing the pause button so the whole scene stops.

Step 4: Imagine your adult self now becoming visible to your younger self and no one else. What does your younger self need to hear? Is it some practical advice? Information, perhaps about what's going on for the people around her? Or is it a suggestion for a different way of handling the situation? Your adult self can now tell your younger self whatever she needs to hear, and listen to what she needs to tell or ask you.

Step 5: In your adult self, take a moment and look at that younger self. If those unpleasant things were happening to any other young boy or girl, would they deserve it? No. Does that boy or girl (your younger self) deserve unpleasant things? No. Allow yourself to feel love, care and sympathy for that child. If she needs a cuddle, imagine giving her a cuddle. Let the child know how important she is – after all, without that younger self you wouldn't be here, would you?

Step 6: Tell your younger self that you will always be there to look after her. That she matters. That she does survive to adulthood and does become as big and powerful as other people. That you care about her and will now allow her to get the good things she deserves.

Step 7: When you have exchanged all the information you need with your younger self, you can press your magic button again and restart the scene. Your adult self has once again become an invisible observer. See your younger self acting to get what she needs and how pleased she is when she achieves it.

Step 8: Make a symbolic gesture hugging your younger self and taking her into you. You, the invisible observer, become one with the you now. Enjoy the sense of completion, knowing that your inner self can tell you what you need and that you, with all your adult skills, can work out how to get it.

For Louise, the painful feeling was of being almost invisible and not allowed to speak. The scene that came up in memory was of playing on the floor when she was about four. Just before dinner-time her mother used to tell her, 'Get up out of the way. Put your toys out of sight. When your father comes in, sit quietly in your chair. He wants peace and quiet when he comes home. One word out of you and he'll send you straight to bed.'

While her invisible observer watched the scene unfold, Louise became aware that her mother hadn't stopped talking when her father came home – and he cheerfully talked back. Only Louise's child self had to be quiet *because her mother was jealous of any attention her husband might give little Louise!*

In the counselling room, Louise exclaimed between tears and triumph, 'It was a lie! There wasn't anything wrong with me! I didn't have to be quiet for my dad to tolerate me!' She now realised that her mother had been jealous because Louise was so important to her father. During her rerun of the scene, she remembered how her mother used to go out to bring in the tea tray, and saw her younger self going up to her father for a hug. That triggered a memory of him smiling and cuddling her, saying, 'Give us a love.'

There and then Louise made several decisions. First, she was important. Secondly, there was nothing wrong with her. Having filtered out the fantasy, she knew she was lovable. Thirdly, she was allowed to speak and be listened to, with men as well as women. Fourthly, that if a man didn't consistently show he valued her, she wouldn't go out with him again. By the way, it was several weeks before Louise realised that she no longer felt suicidal. In fact, she was beginning to enjoy life and had already accomplished several small targets, such as remembering all the times her dad had shown care and affection, and accepting an invitation to a party.

I invite you now to run your own scene, giving it a happy ending. If you like, you can work through it with a friend to give you feedback or ideas, or just to be a witness. Make sure you take all the parts of yourself back into you at the end.

You may find you've already made some new decisions about yourself and the positive things you can now do. If not, please take a moment to do this. You can set yourself small, specific, achievable targets in thinking, feeling and behaving to carry out within a set time.

Summary
You can update early decisions about yourself by reviewing old memories with adult awareness. You no longer need Cinderella/ Frog Prince masks, or Hero/Angel masks. You can decide right now that you are lovable, important, intelligent and valuable.

In short – you can change your pattern transfer by filtering out fantasy masks and carrying out new ways of being with people.

6

—

The Powerhouse

Have you ever kicked yourself for letting others manipulate you? The Powerhouse helps you stop being used and start having more power to get the attention you want

Does what you want count?

Congratulations! You've started to replace the limiting beliefs that dictated your old style of making contact with more positive ones. But at this point clients often ask, 'So what do I actually *do?*'

Good question. Often they've spent years believing what they want didn't count, so they didn't dare ask for it openly. Now they've started to allow themselves to be important, so what they need is a tool to armour themselves against manipulation – both their own and their partner's. Could you use one?

Manipulative ploys are all around us – at home, in schools, on soap operas, everywhere! So you may not be aware of more positive ways to get attention. Be comforted! Most people manipulate at one time or another. It's only human. But now you can learn to do something more rewarding.

Why do people let themselves be manipulated?

Three principles underlie all manipulations. First, we are *unaware* that we're doing it. Usually neither the manipulator nor the person being manipulated is consciously aware of what's going on. Paying attention to how you feel lets you use your awareness to do something different.

Secondly, believing your feelings don't count leaves you open to manipulation.

Although it's easier to blame the other person for doing all the manipulating, often people unconsciously let themselves be manipulated. After all, it does get you some attention, even if time after time it doesn't come out how you hope it will. The feelings you get are intense, whether you generate them yourself or you're treated to a display of your partner's feelings. As each manipulation failed, you'll have felt even less like what you want is important. The solution is to learn to trust your feelings.

Thirdly, it takes two to tango. People who unconsciously want manipulative contact somehow attract others who unconsciously believe they have to manipulate to keep contact. Once you don't need manipulative contact, you won't get sucked into it. And you won't attract partners who manipulate.

With the techniques you've learned so far you're already discovering that you're allowed to *feel* more important. There'll be more on changing the way you *think* in the next chapter. In a moment you'll see some practical suggestions about what you can *do*, but first let's see how a real-life couple rescued their relationship by finishing with manipulation.

What happens if you act like your feelings don't matter
Ginny, who was twenty-seven, came to counselling because she wanted to save her relationship. Her boyfriend Al refused to come with her, but that was OK. Once she'd realised she couldn't change Al but she *could* change her own behaviour to get something different, she started to feel better about herself and more hopeful for their relationship.

Five weeks into counselling, though, she arrived tearful because she and Al were having a row. It started when Al watched a televised cricket match in bed while she was trying to sleep. He spilt beer on the sheets. She was blameful but he said he'd change them the next day. However, when she arrived home exhausted the next evening, he hadn't changed the bed because he was still watching cricket. He promised to do it when the match finished. Ginny exploded, 'You always say you're going to help but you never do!' Al got angry. She called him a selfish, useless slob and stomped off to do the chore herself. Ginny felt disregarded but smug because she wasn't a slob. After an uncomfortable evening, Al gingerly offered her a hug. Ginny pushed him away so he was hostile in return. He blamed her for guilt-trips and she blamed him for selfishness.

In counselling, Ginny wept because she now felt utterly worthless and likely to be abandoned – although she took bitter comfort in seeing Al as a neglectful slob she'd be better off without.

What stopped Ginny from taking assertive action was her feeling that what she wanted didn't count. (In case you haven't spotted it, what she *actually* wanted was Al to respect her wishes and let her sleep instead of watching cricket in bed, and more, to pay her some attention instead of 'putting his cricket before her'. But this is the part she didn't think mattered enough to tell him.)

From a distance, it's easy to see how Ginny put her own crown of thorns on her head. Rather than changing her own behaviour, she continued to feel helpless with Al so instead she talked to her friends about how thoughtless 'men' are. She was comforted because her friends had similar tales. Do you recognise this picture?

I'm not taking Al's part. There are things he could have done differently. But Ginny's strategy of guilt-tripping Al had backfired. Now she was the one who felt ashamed, loveless and worthless.

Blame, shame and guilt are often the way into manipulative contact, whether you're applying them to yourself or somebody else. However justifiable you may feel they are, *they don't work.* Far from getting you what you want, they usually prompt resentment and bad feelings in yourself and others. If you have low self-esteem, these bad feelings may be the payoff because they seem to confirm a world view where everything goes wrong and you're not good enough to get what you want. Even if manipulations apparently work in the short term, they keep the situation static or make it worse.

Here are the techniques Ginny learned to avoid manipulations.

The Powerhouse
The most powerful tool for refusing to accept what you don't want and getting what you do is acting on your feelings. That's your **Powerhouse**. Here are some ways to apply it against specific manipulations.

Emotional blackmail, blame, shame and guilt-trips
These are pleas for emotional nurturing as well as practical attention. Any emotion a blackmailer does receive is hollow, short-lived and full of resentment.

Emotional blackmail feels uncomfortable to the point where you may want to give in to get short-term relief. A better plan is to say something like, 'I feel uncomfortable doing what you want right now.' You might suggest a compromise or a put-off. If someone makes threats, keep your safety in mind. If a person threatens self-harm to 'make' you do something, consider calling a doctor, their parents or some other authority figure. What he does is not your responsibility. You may be able to say, 'That's your choice,' and walk away. If you let him blackmail you once, he'll do it again.

Acting helpless and pathetic

As a means of getting attention, constantly looking to others for help actually earns adults contempt. People are liable to avoid anyone who makes a lot of silent or self-pitying demands.

It's OK to ask openly for help when you don't know how to do something or you physically can't do it. If your partner's capable of doing it for herself you can say, 'I'll help you this time but next time you'll have to do it yourself or get somebody else to help.' And mean it. If necessary you could make an excuse, put her off or act even more helpless than she is. And you can build up your skills!

Asking for help and not accepting it

Lots of people do this. When you make a helpful suggestion they say, 'Yes, but . . .' Their underlying desire is for attention. If the problem were solved they wouldn't know how to get the attention. When you give up trying to help, you feel frustrated and the one who'd asked for help feels angry and abandoned.

What this person really wants is a sympathetic listener. If you're the one that's been asking for help but refusing all suggestions, have you been indulging in a case of 'poor me'? If you have, that's OK. It's fine to have a good wallow now and again. After that, it's time to find out how to fix the problem – and fix it!

Being a magic wand

This is the other half of 'poor me'. Some people always want to fix things so others will be grateful – but never for long enough. Magic wands become martyrs while their partners may develop feelings of inadequacy.

If someone relies on you to the point of taking advantage, you might ask yourself, 'Was I trying to be a magic wand?' and if so, what you hoped to get by that. What you probably *got* was to do more than your fair share while others took it easy. Did you feel good about that? If not, you can now allow others to be adults too.

Mind-reading

This is generally used more by women. A mind-reader does something which they guess their partner will like. In practice the partner might not like it, or feels smothered, misunderstood and criticised. Instead of the attention the mind-reader hoped for, she feels unappreciated and the partner doesn't understand why.

If you keep feeling hurt when your efforts are not appreciated, do you really want attention? You're allowed to ask for reassurance, hugs and kisses! Ones you've asked for count more because your partner thinks enough of you to do what you want. Instead of mind-reading your partner you can ask, 'Is there anything I can do for you?' – and you can believe the answer after only one check-up ('Are you sure?').

Wheedles and empty promises

Remember the playground saying, 'I'll be your best friend'? It wasn't true. In adult life, wheedles and pleading may keep a person in contact with a partner but they engender anger and possibly self-loathing once the partner realises she's let herself be conned. Over time this can lead to distance, painful emotional dramas or break-ups.

A wheedler will not keep his own promises because obviously he thinks empty promises work. If he keeps pleading, it's because it was something you instinctively didn't want to do, or you'd have said yes straight away. If you didn't want to do it then, do you really want to do it now? You can calmly repeat, 'No (thanks).' Or make an excuse and leave.

Flirting to get something

This may work briefly but it can be dangerous. The flirt might feel it's harmless fun but once the come-on stops the other person might feel conned. Anger, contempt, rape and violence are possible consequences.

Real flirting's fun, so long as you both agree how far to take it. Flirting only to get something is a mild form of prostitution. Do you really want someone haggling over your price? And if someone keeps flirting with you only to get something, do you want to let yourself repeatedly be used?

Bullying or yelling

This may temporarily cow the other person into submission, but it builds up resentment and can lead to threats or violence. The bully's partner often loses self-confidence and may come to doubt their own experience. Bullying escalates if you accept it.

You don't have to believe anything bad about you that a bully says. It isn't true. It's only said to hurt. Find any evidence to the contrary, and ask your friends their opinion too. What the bully does, feels and thinks is not your responsibility, it's hers. The prime consideration is your safety. Often bullies will need professional help – *if* they want to change. If it's safe you can stand up to them. If not, you might consider getting help or leaving your relationship, at least until you've both sorted things out.

More serious levels of manipulative contact mean the people involved are unlikely to gossip about what's gone on. If, for example, Al picked up Ginny's shame around her housekeeping and her dread of rejection, he might have told her she was was a worthless slattern who couldn't keep a man. If Ginny now hooked the situation into her innermost dreads she'd hope no one else found out. She might escalate her martyred caretaking while constantly undermining his abilities.

The most intense levels of manipulative contact have serious effects. Sufficient escalation might end in violence, destruction, legal battles or serious emotional problems.

Nobody has the right to bully anybody else. Whatever you may do or not do, you cannot *make* others abuse you or *provoke* anybody into violence. Their response is their choice and you can get help. (See 'Resources')

Now that you've discovered some of the manipulative ways of staying in contact, here's a checklist so you can see if you've experienced any of them. I invite you to complete each line with the name of someone you know who uses these manipulations. You may find that your relatives (or you!) manipulate this way. It's not your job to correct others, though! With adults you're only responsible for yourself, remember?

Emotional blackmail, blame, shame and other guilt-trips
Acting helpless and pathetic
Asking for help and not accepting it
Being a magic wand
Mind-reading
Wheedles and empty promises
Flirting to get something
Bullying or yelling

Right now you may be experiencing a lot of anger towards others or yourself. Properly managed, anger is a good thing because it gives you the energy to defend yourself. In later chapters you'll find some healthy ways to reduce your anger and deal with it constructively.

The Powerhouse in action
Ginny realised she'd attempted the following manipulations: she'd blamed and shamed Al; yelled; expected him to mind-read her need for attention; asked for help without accepting it; taken on Al's responsibilities; and not given him the chance to show he wasn't making empty promises so she guilt-tripped him some more.

Realising this in counselling, her first response was to get into a guilt-loop which left her feeling worse. Then she remembered she'd always hated her mum guilt-tripping her. Knowing she didn't like it, she decided to stop doing it to Al – or to herself. Guilt and blame didn't work.

In order to claim her power she decided to believe her feelings mattered and use them. From now on she'd tell Al calmly how she felt and be specific about what she wanted. She'd also apologise for her half of the row. In the next chapter you'll discover how she untangled her thinking to get rid of guilt and blame. Their relationship was reborn!

Do you want to keep getting hurt in manipulations? Are you now willing to believe your feelings matter and that you have a right to ask for what you want? I hope so!

Summary

Underneath manipulations is a plea for attention. Acting on your feelings is your Powerhouse. This gives you power to recognise and steer clear of manipulative contact. You're allowed to ask up front for what you want and negotiate to get it. If you're still prey to guilt, shame or blame, the next chapter shows you ways to deal with them.

7

—

The Reality Key

Have you ever felt powerless in relationships? With the Reality Key you can expand your personal power

Feeling is not fact

Now you've discovered the feelings underneath manipulations, you have alternatives in what you do. However, you may still be left with some uncomfortable emotions.

Some feelings are good survival tools. 'That hurts so I won't do it any more' is helpful. But when *feeling* gets mixed up with *thinking*, neither can give you a clear message. The results may be depression, anxiety, guilt, blame, shame or hopelessness. When you separate *feeling* from *thinking* you'll discover how to minimise hurtful emotions, and your new clarity of thought will help you solve problems so you have more power in your relationships.

The Reality Key

Feeling and thinking are not the same. Sometimes people wrongly use them to mean the same thing, but *feeling* relates to physical and emotional experience, and *thinking* is about facts. Ten minutes is one-sixth of one hour. That's a fact, not just to you but to everybody else. If you're waiting for your lover to arrive, ten minutes may *feel* like an eternity – but it's not.

Feeling your emotions and thinking about facts both give you useful information but as you see, blurring them can lead to confusion and pain. Mixing up feeling and thinking had helped Ginny stay stuck with uncomfortable emotions. Here's how she untangled her feelings from her thinking to increase her personal power still further. Are there situations in which you'd like to do the same?

Applying the Reality Key to develop personal power

Turn obligation into choice

Ginny had been telling herself, 'I *should* change the sheets', meaning there'd be something wrong with her if she didn't. She'd have failed somehow so Al would reject her. When I invited her to replace phrases like *should, had to* and *ought to* with *could*, she stopped punishing herself with her old beliefs. By saying, 'I *could* change the sheets but I've decided to leave it to Al after the cricket but before dinner', she allowed obligations to become choices. She also respected Al enough to let him take responsibility for himself.

By the way, when speaking to others, asking them 'Could you change the sheets?' implies they're inadequate. It's more assertive to say, 'Are you willing to . . .?' Negotiating a mutually agreeable time limit means you're both clear about what's wanted.

Replace elasticated time with real time

Ginny realised that telling Al, 'You *always* say you're going to help but you *never* do' was stretching the truth in an attempt to provoke maximum shame. She'd discounted all the times Al had helped her or shared chores. Becoming aware of this reality, she felt more valued and so didn't see his behaviour as belittling. She became more affectionate because she no longer needed to feel angry to protect herself.

I invite you to take a deep breath before saying or responding to *always* or *never*. Do the facts indicate *sometimes?* Why see things as worse than they are?

Switch off your crystal ball

Ginny discovered that just because something's happening now doesn't mean things will always be like that. She recognised that her underlying fear of *always* ending up rejected was unrealistic, unfounded and undermining. Losing her dread let her stop being a clingy martyr and start being more confident.

Why not take account of past pleasure and companionship? You're also allowed to value your potential for doing things differently from now on. Life is change. New people come onto the scene all the time, for work or personal reasons. Lots of them could be looking for a loving partner too.

Take off the blinkers and widen your focus

Ginny realised Al wasn't with her *only* because of her housekeeping skills. Taking off her blinkers allowed her to realise he stayed with her because he loved her for herself. This lessened her anxiety and increased her confidence.

Like Ginny, who had relied on Al to give her a sense of worth, you may have come to the mistaken belief that *only* love can make you happy. Sure, love feels good. (And if it doesn't, it isn't good love!) The idea that *only* having a partner gives meaning to your life leads to a terrible desperation – and it places potential partners under the intolerable burden of having to be your Hero or Angel. I invite you to widen your focus. Personal fulfilment comes in many ways, but the point is, it's you fulfilling yourself.

Replace emotional interpretation with reason

When Al hadn't changed the bed Ginny felt disregarded, so she interpreted Al's behaviour as a put-down. She thought his enjoyment of a cricket match meant she wasn't valuable so she'd over-reacted with martyrdom, sulks and anger. Once she realised his lack of action was not deliberately hurtful, she felt better about both Al and herself.

If you feel badly about yourself you might interpret the actions of others as having some special, hurtful meaning which isn't actually there. You might believe others are judging you when really they're not. If you've ever interpreted an action (or lack of it) emotionally, did you feel worse? If so, I invite you to look at it from a point of view where you feel OK about yourself and check whether the action was deliberately hurtful after all.

Drop the magnifying glass

Because Ginny *felt* neglected when Al watched cricket in bed, she'd distorted reality and viewed each subsequent step in the drama as bigger than it really was. She saw his postponing changing the sheets for an hour on the next night as a sign he would *never* help her because he apparently didn't love or value her *at all*. She thus refreshed her dread of abandonment. Once she realised that these were trivial events which formed only a fraction of their three-year relationship they lost most of their power to hurt, so she was now able to take in the positives.

When your self-esteem is low it's easy to magnify bad things. Actually they were specific and time-limited and now they're past. Unhooking fact and feeling takes a lot of the sting out.

Don't shrink the good

The fact is that Al promised to change the sheets after the match. Ginny discounted this, not giving him a chance to make good his promise. When he risked her wrath and gave her a hug, she didn't see it as a big enough sign of caring. (If she had, of course, she would have returned the hug and felt better, so she wouldn't have cried, so they would have made up instead of continuing the argument.) Once Ginny stopped shrinking the good things about herself and Al, she saw herself as more than a housekeeper and realised Al's many demonstrations of affection were valid.

Good things are at least as important as bad ones! I invite you to spend one minute looking for good things in your life – and five minutes enjoying them!

Put borders round responsibility

Although Ginny blamed Al for being inattentive, she hadn't told him she wanted attention. She was responsible for cold-shouldering him when he tried to make up so he was angry at being rejected and scared to show further affection. She also assumed his responsibility for changing the sheets. When she blurred the borders of what was her responsibility and what was his, she felt hopelessness and despair. Once she accepted responsibility only for her own feelings and actions, she had more power because she could choose what she'd do and say.

In adult relationships, each of you is only responsible for his or her own actions, feelings and thoughts. Blurred responsibility is common in abusive relationships, where the aggressor blames their partner for 'making' them angry or harsh. In reality the abuser is responsible for his emotions and for choosing to commit abuse. He could go for a walk or respond assertively instead. I invite you to take responsibility only for your own thoughts, feelings and actions, and hand responsibility for other adults back to them (although if you are at risk, you can do this silently).

Reject misidentification

Ginny's mother used to call her a slattern if she didn't keep her room tidy. Just imagining Al calling her a slattern renewed Ginny's shameful misidentification with that silly word so she lashed out. When she realised she was more than a single action or inaction she no longer identified with that label or the rejection it implied. The Reality Key showed her she wasn't a slattern who put men off, so she felt more confident and could respond assertively rather than aggressively.

I invite you from now on to label the action, not the person – especially if the person you're misidentifying is yourself! For example, if you catch yourself thinking, 'I'm stupid!' you can replace it with, 'That was a stupid thing to do but I won't do it again.'

Replace extremism with perspective

During their row Ginny viewed Al as a *complete slob* who didn't love her *at all*, while seeing herself as *utterly worthless.* This emotional extremism magnified her pain. Thinking back, though, she found plenty of instances of Al doing chores, showing affection, and of herself being valuable and valued. Gaining perspective with the Reality Key let her feel better about both of them so she could now defuse the situation.

Emotional perspectives can lead you to see people and situations as worse than they are. They're usually a mixture of both good and bad. All the tools above help you gain perspective but a one to ten scale of wonderfulness or awfulness can help.

Results

The results of separating *thinking* from *feeling* were dramatic for Ginny. Using the Reality Key, she was now able to stay in contact with the feelings of self-worth she was developing, and act in the knowledge that what she wanted mattered. She was able to take in Al's demonstrations of affection and ask if she needed reassurance. Because she was getting the emotional contact she wanted she no longer needed to guilt-trip Al, so they had fewer rows. Now he didn't feel as though he was walking on eggshells to avoid mysteriously provoking her, so he felt confident with her and they became much closer. Her new-found self-assurance carried over to her work and friendships and back to her relationship in an affirming spiral.

Summary

The Reality Key untangles *feeling* from *thinking* so you feel more confident and act in the knowledge that what you want matters. With more options for behaving assertively, you can get more of what you want. This in turn boosts your self-esteem.

8

—

Your First Aid Kit

If you've ever felt broken-hearted, your First Aid Kit
helps you let go of pain and create a brighter future

Clearing your past history

The last stage in clearing your past history is letting go of old
hurts so that you can move confidently into a brighter future. The
Reality Key plays a vital role in this but it's not the only element
in your **First Aid Kit**, as you'll see.

Odd addition

A neighbour was complaining that her new puppy kept making
demands in her crowded schedule. He chewed her sofa, tore up
her linoleum and woke her too early. She had to rush home at
lunchtimes to feed him and clean up his mess. That meant she
had to bring work home too and she was exhausted. So why not
find him a new home?

'I couldn't do that!' she exclaimed. 'He's always so pleased to
see me. It doesn't matter whether I'm getting on with my husband or not. When I feel bad, I look at Skip and just know he'll
always think I'm the most wonderful thing in the world. I dread
anything happening to him. I love him to bits.'

That's certainly one definition of love. It's a real pleasure to receive unconditional love and admiration. For this timid woman, her dog's love was a source of self-esteem. What she saw when she looked at him was a mirror that reflected her own value. Without Skip's attention, she didn't perceive her own self-worth.

That doesn't mean, though, that her worth would vanish without the dog. She would still be a competent career woman, still have a home, family, friends, interests. Her skills and good qualities didn't begin when the puppy came onto the scene. She already had them, and barring accidents would keep on developing them. What might disappear without Skip would be her *perception* of her worth – and the Reality Key would let her rediscover how valuable she is.

It can be the same with relationships. I often hear the separated, divorced or widowed say, 'Without him I feel like I don't exist any more' or 'Without her life has no meaning.'

I do sympathise. I do understand. When I was younger I used to feel the same myself after break-ups and I hated it. But common as it may be, it's an odd sort of addition.

It's as though 1 partner + 1 partner = 1 complete person. You take one partner away and there's nobody left. It's not true. It's another example of jumbling *thoughts* and *feelings* together so you don't see things realistically. Responding to a skewed version of reality can exaggerate already painful feelings. If you've ever felt this way, the tools you now have will help you untangle perceptions from facts so that you can minimise pain and find yourself once more.

So what else can your First Aid Kit do for you?

Your First Aid Kit

Your First Aid Kit contains remedies for grief, loss (which is not necessarily the same thing), anger and fear. These will help you feel more secure, attract healthier partners and forge more rewarding relationships.

Relieving grief

A degree of sadness at losing a relationship which had some good qualities is inevitable. Sadness is a survival tool. It enables you to know that you have lost something and need to take action to find happiness again. Time can be a great healer, but unless you do something to deal with the sadness you can get stuck in it. Would you want to end up like Miss Haversham, the character in Charles Dickens's *Great Expectations* who enshrined her grief by leaving her wedding breakfast mouldering and cobwebbed on the table?

Underlying her theatrical display was the psychological message, 'I'm going to show you how much you have hurt me until you feel guilty and sorry for me and come back to make it up to me.' I wonder if this strikes an uncomfortable chord with you? I know I and many others have occasionally fallen into this in the past. It's an older version of the playground declamation, 'You'll be sorry when I'm dead.' However, it's one of the manipulative pleas for attention that just isn't going to work. So what does work?

Feeling your sadness is permissible. It's not shameful to be sad. Few people would mock someone who's genuinely upset. Nor would most people be overburdened if you cried in front of them. Everyone understands grief – and it's not catching! They'd probably be glad they could comfort you. They might even feel an increased sense of their own value.

You could take a couple of days off work. In Australia they have a wonderful institution called 'mental health days', although in the UK you might have to ring in sick. During your down-time you're allowed to treat yourself as though you were recovering from a sickness, which, in a way, you are. Comforting foods, drinks, books, videos, phone calls and treats can all play their part. So can creative activities like painting, poetry or music, which help you express your sorrow.

What isn't healthy is to cut yourself off from your sadness. If you don't work through it, it won't go away but will fester inside you. Tears carry grief hormones outside the body, so crying is one of nature's remedies. Also, if you cut off from your bad feelings, you cut off from the good ones too.

Dealing with loss

It helps to distinguish between what you've lost and what you *haven't* actually lost but are afraid you might have. What you have lost is some companionship (though other people can keep you company too). It's easy to get into emotional reasoning and think that your ex is having a whale of a time with a new partner. However, that's very unlikely – even if he makes a big show of it in front of you! If he's behaved badly in one relationship, he'll almost certainly carry on making the same mistakes and getting the same painful results.

When you're dealing with loss, the Reality Key is of great benefit. It helps you see that being sad or alone right now doesn't mean you will always be sad and alone (elasticating time, crystal ball predictions). You're allowed to know that, like my neighbour with the puppy, you are still a valuable human being with good qualities and skills which you can use for your own benefit. Emotional interpretation of the 'He left me so I'm worthless' kind is untrue. You do not have to accept – or give yourself – misidentifications. If you've mistakenly believed that being X's partner was the major part of your identity, it may take some time to re-establish your self as an individual at the centre of your own life. But every tiny success helps.

Some people believe they need to show massive grief as a sign that their love was valid, and think that recovery would somehow be disloyal. This isn't true, either. It's OK to recover from grief. Healing doesn't mean you didn't love your partner. In fact, recovery shows that you have been able to keep the good things about that love. If you need to, why not start telling yourself, 'I give myself permission to grieve and to recover from grieving'?

Sadly, people often think they have lost all the good things they had pictured in their future with the loved one. This is an easy mistake to make, and one that you can rectify. You can still go out. You can still go on holiday. You can still have a laugh. You can still find friendship, companionship and interests. And you can still feel good about yourself. You may take a while to reach this point – but you will recover if you let yourself.

One last point about using the Reality Key to deal with loss: under the stress of a broken relationship, many people look through blinkers. They forget the wide range of pleasures that surround them and focus only on their former partner as a source of happiness. They shrink their own value and resources. Even if your sense of pleasure is diminished for a while, it's worth making the effort to do things you used to enjoy, such as watching favourite TV programmes or going to the pub. It's OK to go to the cinema on your own, or start a new hobby where you might meet other people. Physical exercise helps you get rid of stress hormones and produces feel-good hormones.

Dealing with anger, blame, shame and guilt
Anger is a natural part of our response to loss. You may feel rage against your God or the universe for permitting your loss. You may feel angry with your ex because she is no longer with you. This is also normal for bereaved people, who may feel their partner has abandoned them, and if you experience this you don't need to feel guilty or ashamed. Some people feel angry that other people are going around in apparently happy couples. You may feel angry with yourself for 'causing' or 'allowing' your loss.

In many cultures children, particularly girls, are taught not to show anger. As they grow up they may decide to pretend they're not angry, or be afraid that it is some external force which will overwhelm them. Anger, as we've seen, is a normal pro-survival tool, and you can use it safely.

Again, the Reality Key helps you see where you may have blurred responsibility, perhaps blaming yourself for everything or demonising your ex. You can move away from inappropriate blame and shame, and decide to behave differently now you have more choices.

Revenge, by the way, might initially feel satisfying, but what it actually shows is the power the other person had over you. Isn't stooping to it beneath your dignity? Wouldn't a calm, polite front be better for your self-respect? Your best revenge is moving on to happiness.

To express your anger safely, it's useful to decide that you are not going to hurt yourself or anyone else, or destroy anything of value. Instead, you may choose to shout or hit cushions. Although you may initially feel foolish, it's a great release if you let yourself get into it. You could tear up old letters and photos, though you might want to hang on to one or two so that later you can enjoy remembering what was good.

Another technique for managing anger is to write a letter that you'll *never* let anyone see. Whether the person you're angry with is dead or alive, you can express your rage, recording it on tape if you prefer, so long as you don't let anyone else hear it. You can be as vitriolic and abusive as you like because this is private. Then you put it away for a few days, make a second version that's a little calmer, and again put it away for a while. Lastly you create a final, polite, assertive version that sets out what you didn't like and what you want done about it. Whether or not you choose to let anyone read or hear this is up to you. Then you safely destroy the bitter drafts, which in itself can be quite therapeutic.

Forgiveness is the last stage of dealing with anger. This doesn't mean you have to forget what you or your ex have done. You can forgive yourself because you did the best you could at the time *and you are still learning.* Forgiving the other person is not for their benefit. It's for yours, because ongoing anger can be corrosive and draining. You might even feel sorry for your ex because he was trapped in a way of thinking that either he couldn't help or that will inevitably lead to his future unhappiness. Your ex may feel you are heaping coals of fire on his head if you forgive him outwardly, but inward forgiveness is fine too. If you don't feel ready to forgive yet, you might tell yourself, 'I am willing to want to forgive X.'

Overcoming fear

When a relationship finishes, the three main fears that might arise are (a) will I always be unhappy and alone? (b) will I be able to cope? and (c) what will other people think of me?

The Reality Key shows you that the answers to the first two are (a) no and (b) yes. There are plenty of men and women looking for partners out there, and being on your own has its own rewards. Even if you have to learn new skills like balancing a bank account or cooking, you will cope. Developing new abilities will add to your confidence and independence.

The third question, 'What will other people think of me?' is based on emotional reasoning. One of my clients, a divorcee, expressed this fear very clearly when she said she felt as though she had 'Reject' stamped on her forehead for all the world to see. Obviously this wasn't literally true. She came to realise that her boss valued her because she was competent. Some of her male colleagues were glad she was available because she was a nice, attractive woman. Her friends thought she was a delightful person who hadn't deserved poor treatment. Her family were supportive and angry on her behalf. She now has fun, goes out on dates when she wants to, and is enjoying her life – including adventurous pursuits her ex hadn't wanted to share – while she explores different relationships. She chose to put an end to her unrealistic dreads.

Summary

Splitting up with someone doesn't mean there's anything wrong with you. It just means you can now rebuild a supportive sense of identity. If you want, you're now available to find a partner you can be happy with. You are allowed to recover and you can support yourself through your recovery by acknowledging your feelings. You can also use clear thinking to solve your problems.

Your Safety Net

If you've ever thought love hurts, here's some good news

The **Door to Love** shows you how you can let good love into your life.

The **Definition of Good Love** explains what it is.

If you've ever felt desperately needy, the **Wheel of Life** shows you how to be more centred in yourself.

9

—

The Door to Love

If past experience has led you to believe that love hurts, the Door to Love shows you how to let good love into your life instead

Why do people say 'Love hurts'?

Even without old dreads cluttering your thinking and feeling, you may be half-expecting love to hurt. One reason is *unrealistic expectations*.

Have you ever suffered from any of these fallacies?

Unrealistic expectations

You're never angry with your True Love

Not true. You're two separate people and unless you're clones you're bound to have some differences of opinion. Nevertheless I get letters to my on-line problem page saying, 'Until we had a row I thought this was love.' If the row didn't cause lasting harm and you both felt safe saying what you wanted, you've reached a point where intimacy is OK. If violence or emotional abuse was involved, you may want to consider changing – or whether this is the relationship for you.

You never fancy anyone but your True Love

Another myth! Attractive men and women don't vanish off the planet because you're in love. The difference is that you no longer want to *do* anything about it. Plenty of partners who have loved each other contentedly for years spice up their sex-life by secretly fantasising about pop-singers or film-stars. Because these people love their partners, they wouldn't indulge in anything but the mildest of flirtations in real life. And they certainly wouldn't flirt openly with the intention of provoking jealousy. True love doesn't need manipulations.

It has to be love at first sight

You might find someone's public persona instantly attractive. You don't really know anything about them, though, except that, like you, they're probably on their best behaviour. In real life villains don't wear black hats to distinguish them from good guys. Real love at first sight is rarer than winning the lottery. It's back to those projected masks again.

I'll know him the moment we meet

Many's the client who's said to me, 'I quite like X but I'm not going out with him because I don't think he's The One.' How do you know if you don't give him a try? And if you don't, are you just going to sit around bored and lonely instead? A date is a couple of hours that you just might enjoy. It's not an eternal commitment.

Real love smooths all paths

Untrue. There will still be good times and bad times, bills and sickness, floods and war. Having someone on your side can make life easier – but are you expecting your partner to be your Magic Wand?

The course of true love never runs smooth
Sometimes it does. Sometimes it doesn't. Don't use this as an excuse for putting up with poor treatment from your partner!

There's Only One True Love for me
Another damaging myth. You could have a very happy life-long relationship with one partner – but you could also have a different very happy life-long relationship with someone else. As contentedly repartnered people everywhere will gladly point out.

My True Love will appear out of nowhere
Knights may hack their way through the enchanted forest to awaken Sleeping Beauty – but not in real life. If you never go anywhere to meet people and make new friends, how can your future partner know you exist?

We will get together when it's possible
Mistresses who've spent decades waiting for their married lovers to leave their wives 'when the children are adults' have discovered that it rarely happens. Promises of commitment are useless without actions that follow through in a realistic time-span. If after a year to a year and a half your partner isn't willing to act on a commitment, maybe you need to build up your self-esteem so you can find someone who is available. Or have you actually felt safer with the *avoidance* of true intimacy?

Love is an irresistible force that overwhelms you
Well, no. Infatuation might seem irresistible for a while, especially if you're looking for an Angel so you can feel like a Hero, but real love is both a pleasure and a decision that you jointly take to maintain that wonderful feeling. It's wiser to take things a step at a time. You can trust real love. It won't go away.

What sort of attention are you willing to accept?

So much for the myths. But what about the sort of love you're willing to accept?

Some people actually expect painful attention or feel more at home with it. It fits their experience. This is quite common.

Have you unconsciously been doing this? Do you feel uncomfortable when someone pays you a compliment? If a partner says, 'You're great', do you instantly think she's insincere or patronising?

In other words, do you find it difficult to accept positive attention? If so, how do you expect to be able to accept good, nurturing love?

Attention – what Transactional Analysis therapists call *strokes* – comes in four styles.

- *Positive unconditional* attention is when someone accepts you totally. 'I love you' is a positive unconditional stroke. So is 'You're wonderful!'

- *Positive conditional* strokes mean that someone likes an aspect of you or your behaviour. 'You did that really well!' is a positive conditional stroke.

- *Negative unconditional* strokes are global condemnation. 'I despise you' is a negative unconditional stroke.

- *Negative conditional* strokes relate to specific aspects of you and your behaviour. 'I don't like your haircut' is a negative conditional stroke.

There are different degrees of intensity in giving strokes. The verbal examples above might be modified by expression, tone, or different words. 'Not bad!' might be a weak positive conditional stroke. Said sarcastically, it could be a negative conditional stroke. Yelling, 'You're hopeless!' would be a strong negative unconditional stroke. Emotional abuse may be powerful or relatively harmless – but it's still emotional abuse.

Strokes can also be physical. A caress and a slap are both forms of attention.

Strokes don't necessarily involve touching or speaking. If someone gives you a friendly wave from across the street, that's a positive stroke. Helping you out can be another non-contact positive stroke. Deliberately doing something to upset you is a non-contact negative stroke.

It's true that strokes aren't always given sincerely. The sort of back-handed compliment that has a sting in its tail – 'You did that quite well, for a change' – feels like a prize someone's snatched from you. Alternatively, if a person gushes at you like a luvvie, you may take what they say with a pinch of salt.

But assuming the attention has been given sincerely, what do you do with it? This depends on two things: your self-esteem and your cultural patterns. If you come from a stiff-upper-lip British background, you may have been conditioned to feel a hug is an embarrassing intrusion. If you're from, say, a Caribbean or Mediterranean culture, you may feel that lack of physical contact is cold or rejecting, even if it's not meant that way. So it's worth being aware of these differences.

But self-esteem is often the deciding factor in how you accept attention. Let's start by dealing with how to accept positive strokes.

Compliments are only one form of positive attention. Dismissing them out of hand is an insult to the giver's honesty or taste. A simple 'Thank you' is a graceful way to accept a compliment. But what do you do with positive messages inside yourself?

Supposing someone says to you, 'You're really attractive.' If you don't think you are, you might discount the compliment.

That doesn't mean you're *not* attractive. It just means you're not prepared to consider the possibility. Self-supportive options would be to check it out with a friend; to see whether other people with your various attributes – hair, skin, body-shape or whatever – are considered attractive; or to accept that in the eyes of the speaker you *are* attractive. And if one person thinks that, so may others. Including you.

On the other hand, if you already feel OK about how you look, you might think the compliment valueless. You might have preferred someone to say you're hard-working or thoughtful, and thus discount the positive attention. If this is the way you filter out positive strokes, you might consider whether someone would pay you a compliment at all if they didn't like you. As that's highly unlikely, you can accept that you're being valued.

Some people are supersensitive to touch and find even caresses threatening. If you're nervous of even safe people touching you, it helps if you understand why.

Human beings learn their patterns of accepting and discounting strokes in infancy. Pieces of attention are called strokes, by the way, because without physical touch (feeding, nappy-changing or other aspects of well-being) infants would not survive. Strokes become associated with survival and thus with pleasure.

Caretakers use different types of strokes to condition your behaviour. They might give strokes or withhold them. As a child you may have unconsciously decided there aren't enough positive strokes to go around or that you have to jump through hoops to get them. But even busy parent-figures will probably have had time to yell negatives like, 'Don't be daft!' This was probably intended to keep you safe although it may have been for your caretaker's wellbeing.

In the absence of positive attention, you may have decided you're unworthy or that negative attention is more reliable. You may pine wistfully for positive strokes, manipulate for them, or forget you ever wanted them because you associate them with pain. If so, you'll have learned to trust negative attention and to behave in ways that get it – or to associate with people who give negative attention. You might even be wary of any contact at all.

The tools you've learned so far will have helped you update your self-esteem and behave in ways that get you more positive attention. To allow you to take it in more readily, the **Door to Love** gives you some useful permissions. Why not take time to consider how you could apply each one to enjoy getting and valuing positive attention? In other words, to get ready to accept good love. . .

The Door to Love

There's an endless supply of positive attention
You're allowed to associate with people who give it freely. You can believe good things about yourself. It may help to make a note of positive strokes you receive and work out what they mean for you. For example, a cuddle means: you're cuddly, you're accepted, you're likable and valued. You can rehearse this mentally while it's happening to reinforce your positives.

You're allowed to accept positive attention
Yes, you. You can accept it from friends, family, strangers (a shared smile in the street, for example), colleagues and pets, as well as partners. If you need permission to accept positives, you've got mine. I invite you to give yourself this permission. If necessary, pretend you're your own best friend giving you nurturing permissions! You can ask friends or relatives if they'd let you accept positive attention. If they've got your best interests at heart and they're strong enough themselves, they'll give you permission.

You can give yourself positive attention

Knowing you have good qualities is not big-headed and it can be a life-saver. Why not compile a list of your good features? Small accomplishments are still accomplishments! You can reward yourself with what you enjoy. Bubble-baths, flowers or a walk in the park will not be damaging or break the bank. You can also have treats just because you're you.

Positive attention you get by asking is valid

It's OK to say, 'Don't I look good in these trousers?' or 'Didn't I do that well?' While you may get an insincere compliment, at least the person values you enough to say something nice. If your partner says, 'Well, no, I prefer you in the other ones', that's a valuable piece of feedback. It shows she cares about you. Kisses you ask for are still valid kisses!

You don't have to accept negative strokes

Use the Reality Key. If someone says, 'You did that badly,' is it true? If so, you can say, 'Sorry. Now I know, I'll do it better next time,' or 'Sorry. Will you help me do it better?' But if the criticism isn't true, why accept it? If someone insults you, you're more than just that label. A negative in one area doesn't take away positives in other areas. The critic may be jealous or have some hidden agenda. And remember, no one deserves abuse or 'makes' the other person act abusively.

Summary

Finding good love is easier when you open yourself to it. Becoming more willing to reject negative attention and accept positive attention is rewarding. This is the Door to Love.

10

The Definition of Good Love

If you've ever felt love was a chaotic roller-coaster, you can update your beliefs with this Definition

Wasn't that love, then?
Sometimes clients describe their unhappy love-lives and conclude, 'So my partner couldn't have loved me really.' At this point they usually show one of three reactions.

They cap their conclusions with insults about their partner and hope I'll join in. By blaming the other person entirely, they avoid any personal responsibility for making helpful changes.

Or they look away, make a joke or a brittle remark about something unrelated. By hiding from their pain they ignore the opportunity to learn from experience.

Or they weep because they've decided they're worthless and will never be loved. This position of futility limits their options for making more supportive choices.

Please believe me, I'm not being unsympathetic here. I do understand the pain, and remember all three varieties from my own past relationships.

So were these people loved, or weren't they? The awful truth is that their partner probably did love them – to the best of their ability. And the client, who'd blindly hoped that 'this time things will turn out right', accepted the neglectful, abusive or intrusive attentions as fitting in, at least in part, with what they thought love was and what they could get.

Could it be that you too have experienced chaotic love? Have you accepted undermining actions or words as inevitable in love? If the idea that you're entitled to nurturing love challenges your beliefs, you might like to know how people come to act hurtfully in the name of love – and what good love is like.

In the name of love

Right from the cradle we all have certain rights. The right to be nourished, sheltered, cared for and protected. The right to emotional nurturing. The right to be a child, exploring, playing and growing, and the right to enough caring discipline to let us mature into socially responsible adults. The right to have our feelings respected. The right to treatment that fosters self-esteem.

However much parents love us, for practical or emotional reasons they don't always respect our rights. Here are some case histories showing relationship problems that can arise because of this. In each case, the parents really did love their offspring and felt that they'd done their best for them.

As soon as **Anjuli**, a doctor, got married, her relationship ran into difficulties. Her husband **Dani** expected her to do all the caretaking. He became hostile if she 'chattered' or 'kept rustling papers' – that is, kept up to date with research when he was watching TV. Nor did he allow her to be in a different room from him because he considered it neglectful and insulting.

Anjuli's parents worked hard to put her through med school. They were proud of her – but Anjuli felt they'd never had time for her. It seemed they only paid her attention if she did well in her studies, so she'd unconsciously decided she was only valued for her achievements and that others weren't interested in her feelings. Therefore she believed her feelings were 'wrong' and unimportant. Her parents were delighted when she got engaged because Dani was a well-off company manager. Anjuli felt she coped very well with his 'work-related' absences. She cut off from her hurt and loneliness by working or decorating their home.

Dani's mother was addicted to tranquillisers. At times she smothered him with love, but he felt it was only because she needed him to take care of her emotionally. When she felt frustrated she would take out her rage on him if his father wasn't there to protect him. His mother blanked out these episodes, exclaiming, 'How could you think I'd do anything to hurt you? I love you!' His father worked day and night, and when he did see Dani he alternated between kindness and criticism. Dani became accustomed to negative attention, and mistrustful of affection. While some of his absences from Anjuli were work-related, many of them were drinking binges which he covered up out of shame and fear that she'd leave him.

While both sets of parents truly felt they'd done their best for their children, making great sacrifices under difficult conditions, the way they'd expressed their love hadn't felt good to their kids. Now, despite loving each other, Anjuli and Dani found they were replaying childhood strategies of trying to win or avoid attention while staying safe. Fortunately, in counselling, they learned they deserved safe, nurturing love which they could accept and trust. Despite some bumps in the road, they're now happy.

Other examples of chaotic love include:

- The father who was horrified when he started to find his teenage daughters attractive. Because he loved them he wanted to protect them from himself. From playing cheerful rough-and-tumble games with his little girls, he became cold and distant. They grew up expecting love to be inconsistent.

- The mother who smacked her children with a wooden spoon if they became 'clingy' – that is, if they needed affection. She believed she was showing love by 'toughening them up' since she perceived the world as a harsh place. They associated love with pain.

- The widow who did everything for her son, including making decisions for him because 'she knew best'. He eventually married a domineering wife and ended up spending a fortune on attempts to relieve his psychosomatic pains. But he wouldn't hear a word against his mum because she loved him . . .

Most parents think they couldn't have loved their children more – although their love frequently comes across as damaging rather than nurturing. Their feelings did not translate into behaviours which the child experienced as loving.

No love to spare

However, sometimes even parents who are doing their best have such problems themselves that they have no attention to spare. This may not be deliberately cruel or neglectful – although it may feel like that to the child.

If a birth is difficult, the mother has little support, or there are many demands on her time, the mother may come to shunt the blame for her feelings of inadequacy onto the child because she cannot handle them herself. This can happen with fathers too. Sometimes such children receive the message, 'I wish you'd never been born' or 'I wish you were dead.' Whether this is ever said or not, the child is likely to grow up feeling worthless and unlovable, and so expect love to be painful or scarce.

In some families, either boys or girls may feel unwanted because of their gender. This sometimes leads to their accepting abuse because they believe people of their sex deserve nothing better.

Sometimes parents feel too insecure to admit they can't cope. When problems arise they may scapegoat one of the children. Another child in the family may have the 'good child' role or have to act as a surrogate parent to younger siblings or to the parents themselves. The scapegoat may believe he is intrinsically unlovable. Meantime the child with the parental duties automatically expects to accept responsibility for others' wellbeing, seeing it as more important than her own.

It is not within the scope of this book to address abuse. If you have experienced abuse, counselling is by far the best option; information and contacts are given in 'Resources' on page 249. You did not deserve to be abused. The responsibility for the abuse was not yours. You didn't bring it on yourself or cause it. The counsellor will not blame or judge you. You did what you had to do to survive and I congratulate you on surviving. You can learn to change how you feel about yourself and others.

Dealing with past hurts
If you've worked through the earlier chapters, you'll have started to overcome your old, undermining beliefs and build yourself more support. However you experienced the emotional upsets of your upbringing, your pain was real. Whatever cards you were dealt, as an adult you are allowed to let them go and deal yourself a winning hand. You were not responsible for what happened to you as a child – but you *are* now allowed to take responsibility for dealing positively with what you've got.

Updating your view of your parents and yourself
As another step in getting ready to accept good rather than painful love, it's helpful to find the borders around yourself and the people you grew up with. This exercise helps you update your view of yourself and the people around you from your past. I invite you to start by simply reading through it, anchoring your-

self in the present with a drink. You can come back to now instantly just by opening your eyes.

Imagine a young child, the same gender as you but who isn't you. See how small and vulnerable she is, how much she doesn't yet know. See how the big, powerful people around her can make her do things she doesn't want to. Watch what all the people in the scene are doing. How do you think they're feeling? What do you believe they're thinking? Are they automatically right? Is the child responsible for what's happening to her? Or is it the adults, so much bigger and stronger, that the child is supposed to trust? How would you feel if that child went through the same experiences you did? Would you stand by and watch, or would you want to protest? Would you knowingly do the same to a child of your own? Wouldn't you hug and comfort her and tell her she's lovable? Is the child permitted to express her feelings? What decisions do you think she's making about herself? Are they painful or supportive? Can you suggest other, more helpful decisions the child could now make about herself and about the adults?

That's the end of the exercise, but please read to the end of the section before going back and carrying it out if you choose to.

Growing pains

When you were a child, the only family you had much experience of was yours, and the people who held the power within it were your parents or caretakers. They taught you their beliefs about how life is. Back then you had few other standards by which to judge things, nor the strength to protest. They may have loved you as best they could – or they may not have. Whether or not they meant to hurt you, the fact is that they did. Your experience of pain is valid. You may have hidden it under fear, hopelessness or anger – but you still felt it. If, by the way, you cannot remember much of your childhood, you may want to question why.

Some degree of pain in growing up is inevitable. And even needed: 'perfect' parents who give their children everything and do everything for them would end up with kids who would never grow out of nappies or want to leave home! And bringing up children to be responsible and independent means that sooner or later they will leave home. It is the part of a good parent to allow them to make that transition healthily without closing the door on them.

It's *not* disloyal to realise your parents are not the godlike, all-powerful beings you once thought them. Picturing yourself at the age they were when they had you, do you think you'd be god-like and all-powerful? You're allowed to accept them as fallible people who have bad days, forget things and make mistakes. Who get angry or tearful when they're stressed, and sometimes say or do things they wish they hadn't. You're allowed to find in them whatever good you can – but also to acknowledge that there were times when their behaviour was neither fair nor what you wanted. It still may not be.

Updating your view of them to a more realistic, adult perspective may be painful but it can be liberating. It allows you to realise that their point of view is not the only one, nor is it necessarily the right one for you as an adult. You might also discover that they did love you as best they could. Whatever happened, you are lovable. You may need to feel your anger and hurt before you can forgive them. Or you may decide that what they've done is unforgivable. Page 249 of 'Resources' lists books which offer suggestions for dealing with past hurts.

Best of all, you can realise that you were not responsible for what they did. You're separate from them. You are your own, valuable, lovable self.

I invite you now to go back and update your view of yourself and your parents if you feel this is something you can safely do.

The Definition of Good Love

So what is good love?

It's a consistent package of feelings and thoughts which are reliably expressed in word and deed to show that your partner loves and values you and wants you to know you're safe, accepted and cared for. When you're loved in good ways, you feel nurtured, secure and respected. You enjoy the love you're getting. You know you can be yourself, speaking and acting naturally, and still be wanted. Rather than being on an emotional roller-coaster, you feel stable, centred and at peace with yourself and your partner.

Summary

You're not responsible for other people's behaviour (except for your pre-adult children). You can forgive yourself for what you as a child didn't know or couldn't alter. Now you can make helpful, supportive decisions about yourself, your lovableness and your value. You're allowed to find good, stable, nurturing love.

11

The Wheel of Life

If you've ever felt desperate to find love, the Wheel of Life gives you a support system to build peace of mind

The rest of life

So far we've focused only on love and how to get yourself ready for it. In later sections you'll find ideas about meeting, recognising and relating comfortably with good partners.

But love is only *one* aspect of life. It can't solve all your problems or provide all your pleasure. That would be unrealistic for you and burdensome for potential partners. Thinking that love can resolve all life's puzzles is looking through blinkers. It cuts you off from all sorts of other opportunities for fulfilment and joy. You don't *need* a partner to be happy. Whether you have a partner or not, make your most fulfilling relationship with yourself. Love will come when it comes, and you're doing what you can to bring that time closer.

What about in the meantime? If you've felt desperate to be loved, you can't just wish that feeling away. However, if you put some of the energy you consume by feeling desperate into *other* areas of your life instead, the result is less desperation and more fulfilment. This allows you to feel more centered in yourself, less off-balance and needy. And let's not forget that the greater your level of emotional wellbeing, the more you'll attract others who are emotionally healthy.

It makes sense, then, to put some energy into nurturing yourself so that you can appreciate the pleasure of being at the heart of your own life – rather like the centre of a wheel. We'll come back to that further on in this chapter. Meanwhile, let's look at where you are right now.

Where are you in your life?

You exist in your own right and you experience life through your senses. You're allowed to be who you are. You don't have to be perfect. Life is a journey, and while you might want to be perfect when you get to your destination, you're allowed to be the way you are right now. You've been doing the best you can and you're learning new skills and growing all the time. That takes energy, so you're allowed to get off the train, as it were, have a rest now and again, and enjoy the view from where you are. You can trust that you're in the right place on your journey. When it's time to travel on, you can move forward with growing confidence, knowing you're on the right track.

In California there's a phrase: 'Human being or human doing?' What they mean by that is you're as valuable as any other human being. You don't have to achieve constantly. I invite you to take a look at how you spend your time. Do you ever just relax? Or do you feel uncomfortable if you sit still?

Difficulty in relaxing can be a family trait. I know I 'inherited' a measure of this, as well as a belief that worry without taking action somehow controls events. It doesn't! I learned the truth of the saying, 'If you can't affect it or direct it, you might as well think about something pleasant.' Once I began to accept that I was as important as anybody else and deserved as many good things as the next person, I found that focusing inside myself allowed me to unwind. My daughter definitely appreciated no longer having to live with a tornado! Plus I began to develop peace of mind. Could this be one of your goals? Are you willing to give yourself a chance to find your calm, still centre? This exercise can show you how.

Centring yourself

Getting ready

If you experience any discomfort when relaxing, can you identify the feeling? Is it guilt because you don't seem to be doing anything constructive, or apprehension about becoming aware of self-critical thoughts?

If it's worry and you can't do anything right now to fix the problem, why not concentrate on something positive? If the problem goes away or seems less important, great! If it's still there later, you can deal with it more efficiently from a balanced perspective.

Human minds and bodies need down time. It's OK to let yourself just *be* for a while. Are you willing to set aside a few moments right now to start replacing negative feelings with pleasure in relaxing? You may find that ten minutes, or even five, feels threatening at first, but this is a skill you can learn a bit at a time, the way you learned to walk and talk – by practising. If you start with a few minutes a day you can feel proud of building up your new skill.

Centring – Step 1

Even if you never go any further with this exercise, this first step is valuable in its own right. It takes only minutes to practise, and it's helpful as a quick pick-me-up at lunchtime or when you finish work.

Find somewhere quiet on your own where you can sit comfortably with your spine supported. Rest your hands in your lap and leave your legs uncrossed. Close your eyes and listen to your breathing. Allow your breaths to become comfortably slower and deeper. Imagine your mind is a plain, blue, sunny sky. If thoughts intrude, imagine they are birds flying across the horizon. Soon they'll be out of sight, leaving that blue sky undisturbed. You can imagine your outbreath as a gentle breeze hurrying them on their way to leave you in tranquillity.

This in itself is therapeutic. It allows you just to *be* and lets your mind rest. It helps to get rid of stress hormones and can lower your blood-pressure. Though it may seem difficult at first, with practice you'll find it easier to clear your mind. Encourage yourself gently as you learn this new skill. Each moment of tranquillity is an achievement to be proud of.

When you're ready to move again, start by opening your eyes and looking around. Moving too quickly might make you dizzy, so wriggle your fingers and toes for a breath or two. Then stretch your arms, shuffle your feet and bounce your legs gently up and down. When you're completely awake you can begin to move slowly into action. I invite you to try it right now.

Centring – Step 2

Once you've started being able to clear your mind, why not go one step further? This part of the exercise allows you to centre your mind in your body and achieve a feeling of calm. Again, sitting quietly and comfortably on your own, allow your breathing to slow and deepen. Imagine your inbreath as a soft, cleansing light like a warm, sunny breeze. Picture any tension, pain or anxieties as swirling autumn leaves. Let your inbreath pick them up and your outbreath blow them away into the distance until they're too small to see, the way a breeze might swirl up fallen leaves and scatter them across a park. Each inbreath draws in cleansing light and brings your goals one step nearer.

This too may take practice, but it's worth it for the sense of calm you'll achieve. Don't forget to take time when you've finished to get back up to speed.

Centring – Step 3
After some practice to build up your centring skills, you're ready for the final part of the exercise. Start as in the first two steps. Imagine the warm, cleansing light exploring your body one part at a time. First, your left arm and hand. Let the light of your breath swirl away tension and pain. Two or three breaths should do it. Then a few breaths for each leg and foot. The same for your stomach. Your chest. Your right arm and hand. Your back. Your shoulders and neck. Your scalp and face and throat. All cleansed and healed of pain or tension that flies away like leaves before a breeze. Feel pleased with yourself for getting in touch with your body and nurturing it with cleansing, healing breaths. Again, take time to recover before you move.

Other ways to nurture yourself
Affirmations are positive, uplifting messages you give yourself by saying them out loud, forty times a day, preferably looking in a mirror. They work because your subconscious has no direct connection to the outside world and so can't distinguish between real-time events and imaginary ones. (That's why you can get worked up over an argument that hasn't even happened yet!) All your subconscious hears is the words, not even realising they come from you. Your subconscious can take in positive messages and use them to counteract negative thought-habits, particularly if you've already worked through the self-supportive exercises from earlier chapters.

To show how effective affirmations are, here's the story of **Aimée.**

Aimée was in counselling because she and her fiancé were heading for a break-up. He was aware of her inner dread of rejection and played on it to keep her with him by saying cruel things like, 'You're a complete waste of space. Who else would want someone as ugly and boring as you?'

The tools you've already learned let her realise she was attractive, or she wouldn't have attracted him in the first place. She also became aware that the reason she couldn't talk to him was that he was abusive. Rating her current level of confidence as five out of ten, she now chose to encourage herself to feel OK about leaving him by saying to herself, 'I'm attractive, bubbly and fun to be with. I am now attracting nourishing, supportive relationships.'

Within a fortnight she felt her confidence had risen to seven out of ten. She was already joining in her colleagues' chat and making jokes. Before, she would never have been asked to a hen night. Now she accepted the invitation and found a stranger at the pub flirting with her. This raised her confidence to eight out of ten and she found she increasingly believed her affirmations. Naturally, the more she believed what she was saying, the truer it became. She developed the confidence to leave her fiancé. Now she had a better social life and plenty of dates – though she chose to be celibate for a bit to focus on becoming who she wanted to be.

Affirmations are phrased positively and in the present tense. They don't include words like 'stop', 'not' or 'should'. Earlier you came across the affirmation *'I love and value myself.'* I hope you love and value yourself enough to begin self-nurturing with affirmations! Some examples might be:

I am now drawing towards me lots of nourishing friends.

I am now attracting and creating love in my life.

I am successful and attractive.

I am building more happiness in my life every day.

I am lovable and fun.

You can make up affirmations for yourself, perhaps recording them on a cassette that you can play in the car or while doing mindless chores. They're very effective if you listen to them before you get up or last thing at night. You can also write or type them out repeatedly.

Because you take in a lot of messages from what other people tell you, it's also useful to repeat them in the second person with your name, for example, 'You, Aimée, are bubby and fun to be with.' Likewise you can say them in the third person: 'Aimée's bubbly and fun to be with.'

If you feel any resistance to an affirmation you can start with a lesser version such as, 'I am now willing to start attracting and creating love in my life' or even 'I am now willing to want to accept that I am worthwhile' and work your way up. If necessary you can get feedback from a friend to check whether your doubts are realistic, or you can use the Reality Key (see page 65).

The Wheel of Life

So far we've talked about ways to nurture yourself and put yourself in the centre of your life. You can picture the rest of your life as a wheel radiating out from you. Each spoke of the wheel supports and is supported by the centre. The rim of the wheel forms part of, and cushions, the rest. It's an interlocking support system.

Your life is happening right now. While you may sometimes be tempted to believe your life won't truly start until you find love, it's already under way! Doing nothing but waiting makes time drag.

Do you want your life to be nothing but a waiting room? Why not make each moment more enjoyable? Enrich your life, so that instead of feeling desperately needy, you stay happy and independent whether you're alone or with a partner.

The Wheel of Life offers uplifting possibilities. The spokes of the wheel work outwards and inwards. For example, making your

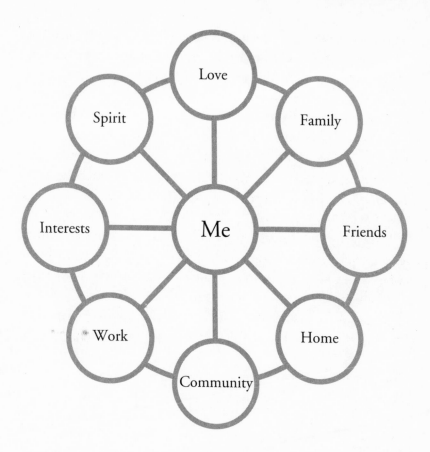

home as pleasant and comfortable as possible is an expression of yourself and how welcoming you are, and a sign that you value yourself enough to make your surroundings comforting. If you value yourself, others value you too.

Giving something back to the community – perhaps helping out a neighbour or taking part in local events – helps you feel rooted, valued and connected. It also extends your social network! Can you think of ways to share in the life of your community? Your local library will offer some good ideas.

Here are those ideas from the Wheel again. Why not come up with something you can do in each of the areas and what it will mean for you? The centring exercise above comes under both 'Me' and 'Spirit' because the spokes work both ways. And you don't have to achieve all your goals at once!

Area	Activity	Shows I value myself because
Home		
Community		
Family		
Friends		
Interests		
Work		
Spirit		
Love		
Me		

Summary

Your most rewarding relationship is with yourself. You're allowed to be at the centre of your life and to make it as interesting, supportive and nurturing as you'd like in as many ways as you can. This is the Wheel of Life.

You and Me

Making Helpful Decisions

Have you ever lacked confidence when it comes to dating? Here are some positive approaches to finding what you want

If you've been frustrated because your partners have wanted something different, the **Relationship Styles Menu** offers a range of choices.

Have you had similar problems with different partners? With the **Type Spotter** you can understand past decisions and find people who suit you better.

If you've ever felt torn about whether or not a partner's right for you, the **Navigator** can help you resolve your impasses.

12

The Relationship Styles Menu

If you've been frustrated because your partners haven't wanted the same sort of relationship as you, the Relationship Styles Menu shows you what's on offer

You and me

Now that you're well on your way to making peace with yourself, it's time to put your head up over the parapet and see who else is out there. After all, relationships are about two individuals.

It's strange, but sometimes people don't stop to consider the implications of that. It's easy to assume that what's been normal for you is normal for everyone. That's not necessarily true. You and millions of others might believe it's normal to want to settle down with a life partner, but not everyone feels that way. There's a wide variety of relationship styles, and some are more appropriate at different stages of your life. Let's see what's on offer.

Love, marriage and changing attitudes

In cave-man days, when life was nasty, brutish and short, survival of the species was the name of the game. As soon as girls reached puberty it was their duty to start bearing children of their own. Considering the average lifespan was around twenty-five, that was pragmatic. It didn't necessarily imply a life-bond, or even love – just practicality. People commonly live in clans so they could share protection and chores as well as companionship.

By the Middle Ages, people had begun to live in extended families rather than clans, though villagers had complex interrelationships with one another. In-laws, aunts, nephews and cousins might all live in the same house. With the advent of troubadours and their songs of courtly love, affection became a stronger motivation, though it did not eradicate bartering brides for land, wealth and titles. Men of rank were educated in war and estate management while women learned domestic arts. While many marriages blossomed into love, the division of interests meant that many couples spent little time with each other. Women were expected to be subservient, with scolds' bridles and beatings maintaining the status quo in the name of the current interpretation of religion.

This shows that romantic love as we know it has only been around for a few hundred years, spreading through Western culture and beyond. Cultures of the Middle and Far East have different mores, though globalisation is affecting attitudes. In some African, South American and Pacific groups, there are plural wives or plural husbands. I well remember a West African woman ridiculing love as a basis for marriage. She said, 'The best thing is to marry the man who brings most fields into the family. Then you take a lover.'

This is not to say one system is better than another. A more appropriate question might be what's on offer and what you want at any given time.

The Relationship Styles Menu

Rehearsal
Nowadays, most teenagers rehearse their emotional and sexual behaviours by having crushes on pop stars or other unattainable figures. The whole point *is* that they're unattainable. For adoles-

cents suffering physical and emotional changes, at the mercy of raging hormones, life is tough enough as it is. Learning to manage your own developing feelings is bad enough without someone else throwing a spanner in the works. In your daydreams you can arrange everything just the way you want it – but in real life your adored one wouldn't behave exactly as you hope. Such rehearsals feel real at the time but at some point you have to draw a line between fantasy and reality. Rehearsal can be a safe, comfortable way of nurturing yourself but keeping unrequited love as your main source of strokes is a recipe for disaster.

The Buffet

Personality traits, while roughly sketched in during childhood and teens, aren't fixed in stone. At fifteen, being captain of the hockey team might be the height of your ambition. At twenty-five your desires, capabilities and tastes are usually different. That means it's OK to practise dating skills, try out different ways of being with partners – and check out whether this is a relationship you might both want to develop. The trick is to realise right from the start that your first love probably won't be your last. You have to kiss a lot of frogs before you find your prince or princess. In other words, whatever age you are, this is part of the selection process. While most religions impose a ban on premarital sex, you may have your own morality. It's worth checking out whether any partner operates by the same standards of morality and discretion. Let's not forget double standards. A boy who sleeps around is often regarded as a daring 'Jack the lad'. Girls who sleep around are often labelled 'slags'. Real gentlemen and ladies don't kiss and tell – or at least, not indiscreetly.

The one-night stand

Some people don't want relationships. They just want sex. If that's OK with both of you, fine, so long as you keep yourself safe and don't have unprotected sex. But do you really want to rack up notches on your bedpost or be a notch on someone else's? If you regret it in the morning, maybe you could boost your self-esteem in a more permanent way. The first section of this book could get you started on that.

The best I can do

If you believe you can't do better or don't deserve someone you love, respect and admire, and if you believe you'll never find someone who loves and values you as you'd like, you might hang onto the first person who asks you out. You could find yourself investing all your emotional energy into a relationship that offers neither fulfilment nor safety, and probably isn't going anywhere. That way lies emotional bankruptcy – especially if abuse is involved. It also stops you getting out, having fun and meeting other people. Time for an injection of self-esteem. Trust me – you can do better!

Kissing cousins

I'm not talking about real cousins here. I'm talking about the kind of comfortable friendship where if you're not going out with anyone else, your 'kissing cousin' is there for you as someone with whom you can go out, have a laugh and maybe share physical affection. If you haven't seen each other for a while, it's worth checking out whether your 'kissing cousin' has now formed another relationship. The affection will still be there but the sexual offer might have passed its sell-by date.

Part-time partners

This sort of relationship used to be the province of people hoping to find the right life partner. Nowadays it's more widespread in all age groups. The main danger is that you may perceive a part-time partnership as an inevitable early stage of a life-bond, whereas your partner may be quite happy seeing you once or twice a week with no thought of commitment or expectation of fidelity. Perhaps he's been too damaged by earlier relationships to want to commit again. Or she just wants some companionship while focusing on her career. Men and women from their twenties right through to retirement complain that their partner keeps them at a distance. It's worth asking early on what the other person's looking for. Warning signs are that she has a string of unhappy partnerships behind her but hasn't made changes; vengeance figures large in her thinking; or she is full of self-pity. Avoid manipulators and agree your ground rules near the beginning of the relationship.

The good thing about part-time partnership is that it can be a lot of fun so long as you both know where you stand. At its best, this can be an adult version of the 'buffet' (see above). After all, it's just a good friendship with a bit of physical affection thrown in, and can do wonders both for your social life and your confidence. Be prepared to move on cheerfully.

The dance of dances
Some dances involve getting closer to your partner, backing off, swapping round and going back to your first partner. It's hard enough to do as a dance. As a basis for a relationship, the on-again-off-again 'dance of dances' feels chaotic to at least one of you. It keeps you off-balance. Even if one of you manipulates the other into making a commitment, chances are this dance will continue on both the emotional and behavioural planes. These relationships often erode self-esteem, so mostly it's better just to leave while you still have the strength. It may be possible to salvage the friendship so long as you put clear markers in.

The engagement
Whether or not there's a formal ring-giving, getting engaged could be one of two things. Either it's a genuine stage of grow-

ing closer, building and earning trust and acting in definite ways that show you're heading for a life-bond. Or it's a long-drawn-out process of manipulation designed to reel you in and keep you hanging around at the distance your partner chooses. If someone says they'll live with you, get engaged or married but doesn't follow through within a year to eighteen months, you may start to wonder whether this is a less obvious version of the 'dance of dances'. If you're feeling off-balance, be doubly careful. Go by what the person does, not what they say. This can also be true when you start an extramarital affair and are told up front that you may have to wait for years for your lover to leave his spouse. Do you want to spend your life waiting for the phone to ring? Do you always want to play second fiddle? Wouldn't it be better for your self-esteem to be out there finding someone who can make you a priority? Or find other ways of fulfilling yourself?

The life-bond

This may seem like your idea of heaven, but it's not everyone's. If you're feeling secure, nurtured and valued, if you're proud to introduce your partner to your family and friends and be known to his, this could be a rewarding life-bond. Be aware, though, that people have very different expectations of marriage or living together. What's normal for you may not be normal for them, remember? There'll be more about checking people out and making commitments later on.

For now, watch out for two indications of potential risk. These are, first, that one of you doesn't let the other fully into his or her life, and secondly, if your partner shows no sign of wanting intimate physical affection. I've known both husbands and wives who'd believed their partners were refraining from premarital sex on religious grounds, when actually it was because they had no intention of ever having sex. All they wanted was the stability of marriage. If they don't at least get turned on a bit or want to pet, it might be time for some questions.

Summary
Any of these relationship styles may suit you at various times in your life. It's OK to date different people and try different ways of behaving with a partner. It's worth checking out what the other person wants and if it matches what you want. The answer to these questions is most clearly indicated by actions rather than words. If it doesn't feel good, you can do something different.

13

The Type Spotter

Have you had similar problems with different partners? Now you can understand past choices and find people who suit you better

A different type of projection

'It was awful!' said **Gwen**. 'I was in my boyfriend's arms and I found myself saying, "Do you love me, Dad?"'

Gwen's story may send a shiver through you, but it's quite common. At its base is what Freudians called 'repetition compulsion'. That is to say, if you haven't received the emotional outcome you'd hoped for in an early relationship, you may unknowingly replay childhood strategies in later relationships, hoping that this time you'll make things come out the way you want. You'll have spotted this repetition compulsion on a grand scale in film stars who marry for the seventh or eighth time, and then seem surprised when it all ends in the courts.

This may all be played out much more subtly than in Gwen's case. You've already had opportunities to update your old beliefs and strategies. But now it's time to look not just at yourself but at potential partners. That way you can understand past choices and widen your range of options so that you don't subconsciously pick people who remind you of somebody else.

Jigsaw puzzle people

You know the theory of jigsaws: for each piece to fit into those around it, it has to have a certain shape. One way of describing a relationship is as though you and your partner were two jigsaw pieces fitting together. So where did that shape come from?

As you grew up, you had to behave in ways that allowed you to survive in your family. Say when you were ten, you cut your arm so badly that you had to go to hospital for some stitches. You may have been afraid and longing for a reassuring hug. Perhaps, though, your Mum told you, 'Be a brave little soldier!' or 'Don't whinge!' This may have been her way of teaching you a coping strategy for emergencies, or perhaps she loved you so much she couldn't bear your distress.

Whichever, the 'Don't feel your feelings' message was probably a verbal reinforcement of what you'd already observed. Perhaps if Mum had a headache she said, 'It's nothing. I'll be all right in a minute.' Dad may have been embarrassed by tears, or irritated because 'scenes' would interfere with his activities. So, as a piece of your family jigsaw puzzle, you'd end up with a notch cut out in the expressing feelings department.

This doesn't mean your fear or your need for reassurance vanished. On the contrary, a worse feeling might now have been

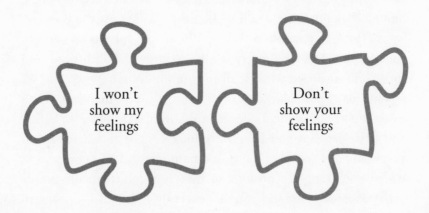

added to the mix: that you didn't matter enough to get reassurance. For your own protection you'd have bottled this poisonous mixture up in a place where you kept similar feelings from previous events. Perhaps the lid you put on this painful spot was built up of decisions like these: that you and your feelings didn't count; that it was 'wrong' or 'weak' to have feelings at all; and that you didn't deserve nurturing.

Notice that the lid kept the feelings in but it didn't get your needs met. That sore spot would still be in you. When you grew up, if you met a potential partner with the same bump of 'I don't like people who express feelings' as your parents showed, you and he would fit together because your behaviours would interlock. It would feel familiar and therefore comfortable because you knew what you were supposed to do. (That's why so many men choose women who resemble their mothers in character, and so many women choose men who remind them of their dads.) Your world view, at least in the expression-of-feelings area, would match your partner's.

But it still wouldn't get your needs met.

When you wanted a hug or reassurance, you'd have some choices. As an adult you might be brave enough to go against your early conditioning and ask for a hug. But your partner doesn't like people who express their feelings, remember? Which means he'd have difficulty expressing his feelings too. You might get your hug. It would still be a valid hug. But would that bit of reassurance be enough to fulfil not just the current insecurity wound but the deeper one too? Probably not, especially since you've carefully chosen a person who not only doesn't like expressing feelings himself, but also dislikes his partners expressing them.

So another of your choices might be manipulation. Perhaps, without being aware of it, you'd cause some disaster so your partner would feel obliged to offer reassurance. Perhaps you'd have a big scene with a lot of name-calling, which is at least a form of attention. Alternatively, perhaps you'd swap straight hugs for a sexual reconciliation.

But your underlying – and ongoing – need for attention is perfectly valid. And it is still unmet. And now you'd be with someone where you could collect a whole new lot of 'evidence' for your beliefs that you and your feelings don't matter, that you're wrong or weak if you ask for reassurance, and that you can't get nurturing.

Of course, people are much more complicated than jigsaws – but you get the picture. People wouldn't just have a couple of notches and a couple of bumps like bits of wood do. There'd be plenty of other painful irregularities, like believing that you'll never be loved, that others will hurt you or that you'll always be abandoned. And there'd be plenty of other people whose notches and bumps would fit right in to keep your uncomfortable belief patterns going. So how do you stop falling into the same trap? How do you spot who will and won't be a good partner for you?

Fairy tales and other myths

Although your personal work in the first section will have healed a lot of the notches and smoothed out some of the bumps on your piece of the emotional jigsaw puzzle, there are still plenty left. Some of them are cultural.

The first is that you can only fall for a certain physical type. The remnants of the old courtly love idea say men have to be tall, dark and handsome, and women should be slim and pretty.

That's all very well if you're Sleeping Beauty, knowing that some prince is going to have to be big and tough enough to hack his way through a Forbidding Forest, and that you're going to have to be light enough for him to carry you off on his horse. Stories like Cinderella, the Frog Prince and so on were designed to carry the message that women shouldn't be independent, because if they're delicate enough (and with small enough feet!)

some guy will come along and take care of them. That's fine if you're in a pre-contraception, bartered-bride society where girls are supposed to stay virgins until their wedding night. But in real life? I think not.

Other parts of the world and other times have different ideals. In Egypt, for example, they sell special fattening jams because plump women are traditionally thought to be more attractive. In 1960s Britain, women were supposed to be stick-thin, whereas now we're supposed to admire big-busted models with wasp waists.

Physical stereotypes give no indication of character.

Fairy tales aren't true. *Tall, dark and handsome = perfect* is bad arithmetic. You can't tell what someone's like by looking at them. You can only tell if they're clean and move confidently.

So what you need is a better indicator. A **Type Spotter**, in fact.

The Type Spotter

I invite you to look back to past relationships and see if you've been drawn to people who share certain characteristics. In the chart below, put an answer on each line for each relationship. One way to do it is to put that partner's initial in a column wherever it seems appropriate. It depends on how you see each characteristic as drawing you to that person.

	Unimportant	Quite Important	Very Important
Body shape			
Height			
Attractive features/ hair			
Dress sense			

	Unimportant	Quite Important	Very Important
Wealth/Power/ Fame/Status			
Socially acceptable (unembarrassing)			
Introduces me to family/friends			
Gets on OK with my family/friends			
Similar background			
Similar intelligence			
Similar attitude to work			
Similar attitude to money			
Similar attitude to spirituality			
Similar attitude to self-development			
Similar moral code			
Similar attitude to the relationship			
Similar attitude to children			

	Unimportant	Quite Important	Very Important
Similar balance between home and socialising			
Similar balance between activity and relaxation			
Similar attitudes to gender roles			
Similar sense of humour			
Some shared interests			
Honesty			
Consideration			
Expresses feelings			
Accepts my feelings			
Openly affectionate			
Kindness			
Generosity of spirit			
Supportive			
Tolerance to stress			
Gives help			
Accepts my help			

	Unimportant	Quite Important	Very Important
Sexually athletic			
Sexually generous			
Sexually close			
Emotionally close			

As you think back to what attracted you to different partners, you may find that you have several initials in certain places and not many (or none!) in others. Once you've got your collection of initials, I invite you to consider whether the areas where you have clusters of answers actually led to good relationships. If they haven't, wouldn't paying more attention to other areas get you better results?

By the way, this is another subject where your perception of what went on is the most important one. Few people will come right out and say, 'I'm dishonest' or 'I'm not going to let you see my home.' They might fudge the issue by making excuses. All the same, if your partner says, 'I can't take you home because it might upset my mother', how are you to know if it's a wife or husband they're hiding? What secrets is this person hiding? Do you want to spend the rest of your life with someone furtive and excluding?

Once again, go by what they do, not what they say. The golden rule is: if you feel uncomfortable with what's going on, this relationship may not be the one for you. It's far easier to break it off after a few dates than to hang on for years, hoping things might alter.

Can you change who you fancy?
Sometimes clients say, 'I can't help it. I just fancy the person/type who's making my life a misery.'

It's true that the protocol – the vague, general outline – for our sexual preferences is laid down in infancy and refined during puberty. It's also true that some elements of sexuality may be determined by the drive for survival of the species. (Back to the big, strong cave-man type with the little woman at the camp-fire!) Fashion, as we've seen, also plays its role, as does the fact we now have fairly reliable contraception.

But just as a Stone Age dweller would have real problems coping with traffic and credit cards, 21st-century people have come a long way from instinctual living. We enjoy the capacity to think and to learn. That includes thinking about what's happening in our emotional lives and learning new and supportive beliefs and behaviours.

It can help enormously to know that, far from being hard-wired, sexual attraction can be reprogrammed. That's not to say there are no good people of the type that you happen to fancy. Therapy is not about taking away choices, but about adding new ones so you don't automatically close your eyes to good potential partners of other types. After all, when you're young you probably don't think romantically of making love with white-haired old grandparents – but most grannies and grandpas still enjoy making love with their partners!

What this comes down to is Rehearsal. A large part of sexual pleasure is dependent on what goes on inside your own head. Good feelings reinforce good feelings. When you meet a potential partner who seems nice but whom you don't automatically lust after, you can try the following experiment. During your Rehearsal fantasies, you might be willing to think about and experience your own feelings of sexual pleasure, and then try transposing one or two of the characteristics of the new person into your Rehearsal. This at least makes it easier to give good people a try. It doesn't mean you have to have sex with them if you don't want to! There's more later about when a good time to start making love might be.

Summary

Fancying some is not necessarily the best criterion for who will be a good partner, nor is your pattern of sexual attraction fixed in stone. As you continue to update your feelings and beliefs about yourself, working out what other aspects of character you find attractive helps you make good choices of partner. And the Type Spotter is a useful guide in seeing whether someone you feel pretty comfortable with might play a bigger role in your life.

14

The Navigator

If you've ever felt torn about whether a partner's right for you, the Navigator can help you resolve your impasses

Have you felt torn?

If in the past you've found yourself torn about whether to stay in a relationship, it could happen again. Here's a guide to why it may have happened and how to make sure it's no longer an issue.

First let's see how you might end up with conflicting impulses.

The patterns we developed when we were growing up are founded on beliefs. In the diagram overleaf, you'll see that that the three interlocking segments, 'Feeling', 'Thinking' and 'Behaving', rest on your underlying belief system. Under pressure, such as during a bad patch in a relationship, people generally assume one segment is less important than the others. Their belief system switches onto automatic pilot and blanks that part out, or fogs it so it doesn't function efficiently. Or one segment might reflexively take over. If you're not getting feedback from all areas you can end up with a big dilemma.

Let's look at how thinking, feeling and behaving interlock. You might, for example, have the unacknowledged belief that you're allowed to be good at thinking about externals like work or academic areas. At the same time, though, you may have the unacknowledged belief that you're not supposed to think about what's going on in relationships. Without being able to think about relationships you might not (a) realise that there is a problem, (b) gather data or make useful comparisons or (c) arrive at a valid solution.

Similarly, if you have an unacknowledged belief that you're not supposed to feel your feelings or that they don't count, you may be unaware that there is a problem, or believe the situation is unchangeable and you're wrong to feel the way you do. This means you won't be able to *think* how to solve the problem or *behave* differently to get a different outcome.

Cycle of Beliefs

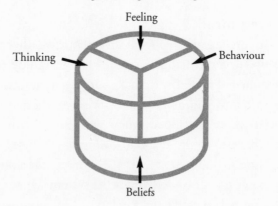

Fogging out feelings means you use up a lot of energy holding yourself in an impasse. While your own experience of such dilemmas may be less dramatic, the processes of getting stuck and how to unstick yourself are the same.

It's the same if your behaviour is automatic, or you believe something is the 'right' or only way to behave. With your options limited or apparently nonexistent, you'll carry on doing what you're doing and getting the same unhappy results.

Feeling stuck

You may remember **Marie**, who stayed in an abusive marriage for fifteen years. For most of that time she covered up what was happening to her out of feelings of shame, inadequacy, disloyalty and guilt. As in the Irish saying 'Angel in the street, Devil in the house', her husband **Nick** was quiet but sociable outside the home and everybody thought he was a lovely man. Though their relationship had always been an emotional roller-coaster with physical fights followed by reconciliations, things changed one time when Marie lashed out. Stepping back, Nick tripped and landed badly, fracturing his wrist. Marie felt terrible as this time it was she who'd instigated the violence in response to emotional abuse. None of their previous fights had caused more than bruises or grazes. After that she refused to 'lower herself to his level' and hit back – whatever he did.

Although she explained this to him and asked if henceforth they could sort things out by discussion, Nick started hitting before talking. As stress at work left him feeling increasingly powerless he began to drink more heavily. On top of his corporate entertaining he now got through a bottle of whisky most nights after a drinking session at his exclusive club. This interfered with his perceptions and his self-control. Boiling pans, kitchen knives and broken bottles all featured in his threats but it was only after a year or so that Marie realised he never actually marked her permanently, or where it would show. Like many abused men and women she wore high-necked shirts, long sleeves and trousers to disguise her injuries. With panic attacks and diminishing self-esteem Marie felt unable to leave, and for years was too ashamed to discuss her situation with anybody else. When Marie finally hinted at discontent, her mother said, 'Good wives don't have problems managing their husbands.' Two so-called friends said she must enjoy the drama of being abused. A male 'friend' took the point of view that Nick was a lovely guy and she must either have imagined or provoked the violence.

Reasons for staying stuck

Marie's reasons for staying in her marriage were many. She would often try to untangle them by writing things out 'logically', although her logic was coloured by her religious and other beliefs. Holding the dilemma was painful and costly in emotional energy. After tearfully writing out her pros and cons she would gratefully repeat her mantra, 'I don't have to decide today.' With her permission I reproduce one of her lists so you can see how her beliefs tangled her thinking and stopped her from accepting her feelings as valid, let alone important enough to act upon.

Reasons for staying	*Reasons for leaving*
Sacredness of marriage vows	Cowardice
Divorce means I'll go to hell	Failure
Status of wife (perceived as) higher than single woman	Disloyalty
He needs me and loves me in his own way	Breaking my vows is blasphemy
Ill – might die if on my own	I'm too weak to handle marriage like other women
My role is to support him	
Would have to leave nice home	
No one else would have me	
It's all right sometimes	
My parents, friends etc. like him	
He's not like this with others so it must be my fault	
Financially dependent	
All marriages are like this so there's no point in changing partners	

It's so much easier to see when you're not in someone else's shoes, isn't it? You can tell that Marie's reasons for leaving were highly judgemental rather than factual. She equated leaving with failure, cowardice and other negative qualities. In fact, it was not until her husband made three separate drink-fuelled attempts to kill her that she actually left – and part of her motivation was to save Nick from prosecution for murder!

While you might have expected her 'reasons for leaving' list to start with 'Nick hurts, frightens and belittles me', her under-lying Cycle of Beliefs stopped her from recognising those facts, or realising how important they were. She only felt the feelings she believed she was permitted to feel: that Nick loved and needed her and that she was responsible for anything that went wrong between them. However, she was ashamed of her pain and guilt, believing she was weak to feel it, so whenever possible she blanked it out. What she couldn't do, though, was stop her body being aware of it. Stress will out, and in Marie's case it came out in panic attacks, migraines and other physical ill-nesses.

With her survival feelings blocked, there was no stimulus to effective thinking. Marie's beliefs had also included the damaging one that while she was permitted to shine academically (she was a lecturer), she wasn't supposed to think about what was going on in her relationships.

This stopped her gathering useful data, such as whether it's normal for husbands to attack their wives (it's not); whether she could finance a nice home for herself (she could); that she could phone a friend, a doctor or an ambulance if she was ill; that attempted murder is a greater 'sin' than divorce; and that she wasn't actually responsible for Nick's feelings.

This limited her options for behaving differently so she believed she couldn't change her situation. She'd suggested coun-selling, treatment for alcohol addiction and self-help books. She believed her only option was to 'fix' her husband. Like a lot of people, she came to counselling initially for someone else's problems rather than her own.

What about you? Are you willing to find a way to resolve your emotional dilemmas, even if it means updating your Cycle of Beliefs?

The Navigator

You may never have questioned the role of your underlying beliefs in dilemmas. You probably thought everyone believed the same things until you began to challenge them with self-help exercises.

Some of these beliefs will be about yourself as opposed to others. For example, Marie knew that other people weren't condemned if they got divorced – but she was convinced she personally would go to hell.

The **Navigator** helped her disentangle her thinking, feeling and behaviour from her underlying beliefs. You too can use it to avoid staying stuck. You'll need to write down your answers to these questions.

1. *How do I feel in this relationship? Is it closest to anger, sadness, fear or happiness?*
2. *Would other people be allowed to feel this feeling?*
3. *Is this my feeling or am I taking responsibility for another adult's actions, feelings or wellbeing?*
4. *Would I like a good friend to feel like this?*
5. *What events are leaving me feeling this way? (Avoid value judgements, emotions and beliefs – stick to observable facts.)*
6. *Might other people respond differently in my situation?*

7. *Do I give myself permission to feel what I feel?*

8. *If it's not happiness, what do I need to be happy?*

9. *Would other people be allowed to do something to change the situation?*

10. *Am I willing to allow myself to do something different to be happy?*

11. *Where can I find objective data to examine the situation differently? (Friends, books, counsellor, police, doctor, lawyer, someone whose judgement I respect)*

12. *What solutions might people I admire come up with?*

13. *Are they ethical solutions? Who can objectively help me find this out?*

14. *What might be the consequence of these solutions if someone I admired put them into effect? How would they handle that?*

15. *How could I deal with those consequences self-supportively? (Again, you can consult your resources.)*

16. *How could I minimise any pain or difficulty I or another person might feel?*

17. *Am I responsible for that person's feelings? (Yes, if it's a child in your care.)*

18. *If I fear others' criticism, are they the ones who are living my life or am I?*

19. *What would I need to carry out any of those solutions?*

20. *How could I get those resources?*

21. *When will I start getting them?*

22. *How might I sabotage myself?*

23. *What can I do to support myself instead?*

24. *When will I be willing to put a solution into effect?*

Results of the Navigator

Using the Navigator to separate and update her feelings, thinking, behaviour and beliefs liberated Marie. Once she decided to admit the truth openly and seek help, her resources included friends, a colleague in the same situation, books, her doctor, a counsellor and the people at a women's refuge. Her brother and parents were supportive and a lawyer helped her with her divorce and settlement. She was hurt that Nick was the first to remarry but he repeated his pattern of abuse and is divorced again. Marie now has a loving husband and nice home.

Summary

You can use feeling, thinking and behaving as a feedback system to update your beliefs about yourself, the world, other people and what's happening in your life. The Navigator shows you one way to do this. This allows you to find and apply more options. In relationship dilemmas, the feedback from feelings is usually the first step forward.

Checking Out the Opposition

If you're unsure whether this will be a good relationship for you, or if you tend to blame yourself when things go wrong, here are some useful tools for checking out potential partners

If you're not sure how to flirt with someone or whether you should, **Silent Signals** will help you give – and get – the response you're after.

Have partners ever behaved in ways you don't understand? The **Detective** helps you check out what's going on and what you can do about it.

15

Silent Signals

If you're not sure how to flirt with someone or whether you should, Silent Signals will help you give – and get – the response you're after

How do I know someone fancies me?
By the time you've reached the stage of wondering whether the person you've got your sights on also has their sights on you, you'll have been through two stages of making contact already. First, you'll have been through the emotional absence stage, where you just eyed him up without making contact. This may have taken months – or seconds. Then you'll have been through the impersonal contact stage, talking about neutral subjects, common interests or mutual friends. Both stages let you check each other out to see whether it might be worth taking things further.

But how do you recognise that someone is interested in you? How do you discover whether they really have partner potential? And what can you do to attract them?

Silent Signals
Body language is now passing into general awareness. While *everybody* communicates with body language all the time whether

they know it or not, being able to read it consciously is a very useful skill. If you're not convinced, imagine you're speaking to someone and they turn their back on you. How would you feel? Without a word being said, you'd receive the message that they weren't interested in you, and you might even decide that they were discounting or rejecting you. Hopefully you'd realise the problem lay with their rudeness and that you're OK.

In Western culture, interest in developing a relationship for even a short time is shown in these ways.

- He looks you in the eye a bit longer and more often than other people might.

- Women in particular may hold a potential partner's gaze just long enough for him to notice, then quickly look away to the side.

- He smiles sincerely at you.

- She faces you straight on and focuses on you.

- He may tilt his head slightly to one side but his chin will probably be level unless he's taller than you.

- She may have one foot pointed in your direction.

- He comes a bit closer (less than 15 inches/38 centimetres) into your personal space than acquaintances usually do.

- She may lean towards you.

- He may have his arms open rather than held across his stomach or chest.

- Men will allow their legs to be open rather than crossed. Women, if brought up to be 'ladylike', might not do this for cultural reasons so this sign isn't reliable for women.

- Women who do cross their legs may point one of their knees at you if she finds you attractive. This is particularly true if the woman has adopted a relaxed posture with one leg folded under her and the bent knee pointing at you.

- If women cross and uncross their legs slowly, this can be a come-on signal, as can slowly rubbing her hand over her thigh.

- Interested parties have their hands open rather than clenched or holding each other (though women may have been taught that it's ladylike to fold their hands in their laps).

- He may touch you lightly on the arm, back or shoulder.

- Women in particular may lower their heads a fraction and look up slightly under their eyelashes at a potential partner (the Princess Diana look).

- Women may give a sideways glance over a shoulder they've raised.

- A man may straighten his tie or smooth his hair.

- A woman may smooth or twiddle her hair.

- Women slide one heel out of their shoe several times and pull it back on again by moving their foot and leg.

- The pupil – the dark spot in the centre of the eye – becomes enlarged when someone is sexually attracted to you.

Nightclubs and some restaurants have low lighting to induce a seductive effect (because it's good for business!).

Other non-verbal signals of attraction

- People hoping to attract your interest lower their voice slightly, perhaps hoping you'll lean closer to hear them.

- The tone will become soft and caressing. Good flirts can make even shopping lists sound sexy! Try mimicking romantic actors and actresses, but don't go over the top unless you and anyone you're practising with want a laugh.

- She'll focus her gaze on a triangle between your eyes and mouth.

- He'll extend the triangle to include your eyes, mouth and points south.

Practising in front of a mirror and then with feedback from a friend (which can be good fun), you can develop skill in flirting.

Some homosexual men love flirting with women, perhaps outrageously. It doesn't mean he fancies her. It's just fun.

Possible warning signs

- Rounded, drooping shoulders may indicate a person who's feeling down. If both shoulders are very rounded or the posture appears habitual, they may be issuing manipulative invitations for you to take care of them. Wouldn't you rather be an equal partner than a Band-Aid?

- People who tap or fidget a lot probably either don't want to be there or they may have issues of anger or lack of confidence.

- People who habitually blink a lot (other than for conditions like conjunctivitis or something in their eyes) may have confidence issues.

- People who blink slowly, more than six or eight times a minute while you're talking, may be focusing on something inside themselves – or they may be bored.

- Closed body language – hands clenched, arms barred across the body – may indicate hostility or insecurity.

- People – especially men – who rock up and down on their heels may be arrogant or attempting to dominate you.

- People who look down their nose at you don't want to know. That's their problem, not yours.

- People who won't meet your gaze for a comfortable length of time or with comfortable frequency may have something to hide – even if it's only nervousness. If it hasn't worn off after an hour or so, you may wish not to pursue this relationship.

- People who look at the floor a lot may have confidence issues or want to hide something.

- People who habitually frown so that there are two vertical grooves between the eyebrows *may* have intimacy issues and be manipulative about asking for attention. If you don't see them frowning much, it could just be that they haven't worn sunglasses on bright days.

- People who cover their mouths often while speaking, even if it's only rubbing their nose or scratching their cheek, may be lying, fearing rejection or thinking they deserve negative judgement.

- A shallow indentation running around the ring finger of the left hand (the right hand in some Continental countries) may indicate a person who's recently divorced and is perhaps on the rebound. This isn't the best basis for a stable relationship! Or she may be trying to disguise that she's still married. You can check it out with casual questions. In summer this dent may be paler than the surrounding skin.

- People who use chat-up lines are not displaying much social skill. Chat-up lines are cheesy. They indicate that the person's interest is probably in 'scoring' rather than relationships or that they're desperate for any partner at all.

- Some people flirt manipulatively to get favours. Unless you both know it's fun, it's tacky.

- Some men flirt reflexively even if their partner's there. This doesn't necessarily indicate that he'll be unfaithful. In some men it's a pathetic response because they're intimidated by women or by intimacy. In others it's arrogance or game-playing to boost a damaged ego or manipulate their partner. This goes for some homosexuals and lesbians too. If your feelings keep telling you it's an uncomfortable situation, listen to them!

- Watch out for a down-hinged tone, where somebody starts a sentence on an upbeat note and then adds a depressing rider, for example: 'Isn't it a lovely day? But it's bound to rain later.' This can be an indication of depressive tendencies or a reluctance to act to get what they want. If it's you that's doing it, put the downbeat part first and finish on a positive note!

Of course, you may have your own perspective on any or all of these points. Some nervousness with new people or in new situations is almost inevitable. This can lead to a degree of body-barring – perhaps fiddling with watches or two-handed holding of glasses or brief-cases – which isn't necessarily a bad sign. If the nervousness persists over more than three or so arranged meetings, the chances are that you and this person won't be able to be as intimate as you may hope.

The clue is in how comfortable you are in their company. If you keep getting that 'on trial' feeling where you fear what you say or do might get you dumped, you may consider dumping them first.

Should women ask men out?

What a sexist question! It's still a debatable point, though. In certain circles, probably more in managerial than other groups, it's usually considered OK.

However, if a man isn't interested enough in you or a relationship to ask you out, having you offered on a plate may keep his attention for a while, but do you honestly think it's a good basis for a stable partnership?

I also get a lot of schoolgirls writing in to ask whether they should ask out this boy they fancy. The girl thinks he's interested but too shy to ask them out. If he's got so little self-esteem that he won't act to get what he wants in relationships, do you think he'll have enough gumption or drive in other aspects of life? And are you sure he won't gossip or laugh if his friends plague you? I've seen teenage girls cry oceans for weeks when boys they'd fancied made their lives a misery.

This, though, is only my point of view. I've heard men say they're flattered if a woman asks them out. Offhand, I can't think of any of them who've actually settled down happily with that woman, but undoubtedly some successful relationships start this way. As an adult it's up to you.

My friend says . . .

Huge amounts of emotional pain result from friends who say, 'So-and-so fancies you but he doesn't know how you feel about him.'

Quite often this is a wind-up but even if it's the straight goods, I repeat: do you want to go out with someone who makes so little effort to engage your interest?

The best answer to those well-meaning (or otherwise) friends is: 'If he wants to know, why doesn't he ask me?' You can make it a bit more light-hearted and jokey by adding, 'I don't bite – much.'

Summary

Over half of all communication is non-verbal. Flirting should be fun. You get better at sending and interpreting Silent Signals with observation and practice and you can set comfortable limits on others' flirting. If they're interested enough to ask you out, they will. If they don't ask you out, either they're not interested, or they don't have enough drive to cope with life, so don't worry. There are plenty of other people who are emotionally available and who'd suit you better.

16

The Detective

Have partners reacted in ways you don't understand?
The Detective shows you a way to check out what's
going on for them – and what you can do about it

Incomprehensible actions
Sometimes people suddenly start behaving in ways you don't
understand. In the past you may have thought, 'I must have done
something wrong', which is probably not true. What's happening
may well not be anything to do with you, as you'll see.

Why did she do that?
Finding out what's gone wrong may be a priority for you, particularly if you're feeling insecure. If you feel your sense of personal
value is at threat, your subconscious could be picking up signs
you don't consciously notice. This applies in both single-sex and
heterosexual relationships but here's one example of bizarre
behaviour to show you what's going on underneath.

Lauren, a divorcee in her forties, had been going out for several
weeks with **Bill,** who had been very attentive. Friends said they
didn't have much in common: she was a piano teacher and he was
a fork-lift truck driver, but they said they'd prove their critics
wrong by building a solid relationship.

One night they arranged to meet in their local pub. But when Lauren arrived, Bill barely spoke to her. He talked to friends or played the fruit-machine, leaving her alone. She felt awkward and wanted to go home but she was afraid Bill, so attentive up to now, wouldn't call her again. What had she done to upset him? Feeling inadequate after her painful divorce, she was determined to hang onto Bill at any cost.

Lauren could only think of staying until closing time and walking back with Bill to his flat. She was uncomfortable with this but too insecure to act on her hurt and go home.

Bill tried to avoid speaking but she badgered the answer out of him: she was wearing a short skirt. He felt ashamed to be seen with a 'tart' and so he'd decided, without telling her, to dump her. It was only when she 'bought' Bill's attention by promising to wear only what he liked that he agreed to go out with her again. He explained it was in her best interests because she wouldn't want people thinking she was cheap.

Even after two years Lauren felt she was on trial. It was another of Bill's inexplicable refusals to contact her that finally showed her this relationship wouldn't ever turn out like she wanted. Weeks later when he turned up out of the blue she broke it off completely.

Lauren's self-esteem had suffered because she'd mistakenly believed Bill's rejecting behaviour was her fault. It wasn't. Piecing it together later, she realised that erratic parenting had left Bill terrified of being rejected. Wanting to please, he could turn on charm like a tap. His fear of rejection meant he didn't want Lauren being so attractive that other men might cut him out. Unable to bear the terrible anxiety of 'waiting for the other shoe to drop', though, he eventually behaved so appallingly that Lauren (and all his previous partners) dumped him.

Desperate for the perceived status of 'Bill's girlfriend', she'd blanked out her feelings of humiliation. In counselling Lauren realised that her meek acquiescence felt like she'd given up her self-respect. As a child she'd had to be a caretaker, mind-reading her father's wishes. Her own feelings had been discounted. This was why she'd felt she fitted in with Bill like two pieces of a jigsaw!

Small inexplicable behaviours are often the tip of the iceberg. So what can you learn from them and how can you avoid getting hurt?

The Detective

The answer lies in applying the **Detective** to your partner – and to your own reactions. Here's how it works.

Your Detective consists of:

- *Feeling:* Trust your feelings. Discomfort is a useful spur to thinking and action.

- *Behaving:* Gather objective data about what your partner's doing. You can ask for information with the emotional literacy formula: 'When you (shut me out) I feel (scared) so are you willing to (tell me why you did this particular thing)?' Either this resolves the problem or you get no suitable explanation. Then you can use your –

- *Thinking:* Apply the Reality Key to your feelings. Are you practising an emotional interpretation of neutral actions? Blurring responsibility? Hooking into past hurts by elasticating time? Getting into crystal ball predictions or looking through blinkers, so you believe only this painful relationship stands between you and eternal loneliness?

The Detective and you

If you're unhappy when someone inexplicably doesn't call or does something unpleasant, the conclusion is not that there's something wrong with you, but that there's something wrong with him. Healthy people explain.

If someone does behave inexplicably, the following are some ideas of what might be going on:

- He doesn't feel confident enough to act assertively.

- She's looking for excuses to avoid intimacy.

- He's being manipulative to get extra attention.

- She's covering up some guilt of her own.

- He has something to hide.

- Her Cycle of Beliefs (see page 128) may be out of kilter, so she doesn't trust her judgement.

- He fears rejection, engulfment, neglect or abuse to the point where his inner experience has more impact than external reality.

- She's protecting herself or someone else, possibly you, from some perceived threat.

- She therefore thinks she has greater power than you do.

You may never know which, if any, of the assumptions is at the bottom of his inexplicable behaviour. It's not your problem or your fault!

This will minimise your feelings of discomfort but they could still be there, and they're there for a reason – so that your *feelings* give you options in both *thinking* and *behaving*. Discomfort is a stimulus to do something different and get a better result.

The Detective in action

Once Lauren unblurred responsibility by applying the Detective, she realised she hadn't done anything wrong. Bill *could* have been assertive and discussed problems with her instead of breaking off communication.

Trusting her feelings of discomfort helped Lauren think clearly. If Bill was worried about other men asking her out, it meant she was attractive and valuable. He acted from his fear of intimacy, not because there was anything wrong with her. The break-up lost its sting. By seeing it as a learning experience and accepting that she'd had some good times, she gave up her feelings of guilt, self-pity and inadequacy.

Although Lauren came into the process too late to improve her partnership with Bill, she now had a foundation for behaving differently in future – starting with no longer tamely accepting uncomfortable behaviour from new partners! She went on to build increasingly rewarding relationships.

So can you!

What's this got to do with picking the right partner?

The Detective is a way of bringing into play all of your Cycle of Beliefs. You can use your thinking, feeling and behaving to check out potential partners. If he refuses to address or resolve problems, you can acknowledge that this isn't the one for you. It's not your job to fix other people! Your self-esteem doesn't depend on another person – and if she is damaging it, why not bow out gracefully before it gets too costly?

Summary

If people behave inexplicably in ways you find uncomfortable, the Detective shows you that it's unlikely to be because of something you've done. Your validity as a human being does not rest on having damaging people in your life. You can use discomfort and other feelings to prompt your thinking and behaving to improve communication, or decide this is not a nurturing relationship. You deserve better.

One Date at a Time

Have you ever been unsure at the start of a relationship? These tools can help you manage the first stages comfortably

The **Date Menu** is useful if you've ever felt at a loss when trying to find decent partners or uncomfortable on first dates.

The **Safe Pace** helps you stop diving in at the deep end and start building security within relationships.

Is this love or infatuation? The **Love Scope** helps you work out the difference before it's too late.

17

The Date Menu

The Date Menu is useful if you've ever felt at a loss when trying to find decent partners, or uncomfortable on first dates

Are you ready for dating?

Now that you've sorted out a lot of your hang-ups, and you know what you want and what you're not willing to put up with, isn't it time to get out there and start looking around?

Rest assured that there are plenty of available partners in every age group. New men and women come onto the scene all the time. They may have recently moved to the area, split up with or divorced their partner or been widowed. Some might simply have decided they're finally ready to settle down. There are potential partners who want the same sort of relationship that you do, and there is also less competition than you might think. And don't forget those who are stuck at home waiting for their Hero to ride out of myth to their door. Be grateful to them. They're increasing your odds of success!

The thought of dating can be scary if you're out of practice, especially if you have recently ended a long-term relationship. But you'll soon get back into the swing of things. The dread is worse than the reality!

It can be a lot of fun. Exciting. Different.

And it helps if you're aware of *why* you might get those open-ing-night butterflies.

Why might the thought of dating scare you?

Various factors may combine to construct your particular brand of nervousness, whether you're new to the game or long out of practice. Do any of the following dreads strike a chord? If so, the remedies are at hand.

What if I'm making a big mistake?

A date is a date. It's not a lifetime commitment. You don't have to decide in the first ten seconds if this is the person you want to spend the rest of your life with. If you feel reasonably OK with them and you have a reasonably good time, maybe you will see them again. If you didn't enjoy it, no problem. It's good manners to stay at least an hour or so. After that you can make an excuse and leave. This is not the only available man or woman in the universe, and your self-worth does not depend on their approval.

What if it turns out badly?

There are degrees of turning out badly. Obviously you need to avoid real trouble, and I've listed safety rules below to help you with that. But for the moment let's look at ordinary not-getting-on-well scenarios. Say it's a blind date and you don't like the look of the person. Having talked with her for a while you may find your prejudices or nervousness were unfounded, particularly if they belong to the 'my type' myths. On the other hand, maybe the Reality Key confirms your doubts. So don't see this person again! You don't have to be insulting, but it's OK to say, 'Thank you for a pleasant evening, but I don't think we'd suit. Best of luck. Good-bye.'

Of course, it's also possible that you'd like to see the person again but they don't want to see you. This doesn't mean there's anything wrong with you. For all you know, this person is in the throes of some incomprehensible inner dilemma. Or married. Or just unpleasant! There are hordes of people out there who *are* emotionally available! Your self-esteem doesn't rest on an hour's encounter with a stranger. And you can congratulate yourself on your bravery in practising dating. Better luck next time.

What if I make a fool of myself?

You're more than just a label, remember? During one first outing, I recall being so nervous that I spilt a glass of red wine all over my date's cream trousers. The glass shattered and it seemed everyone was turning to stare. Some of them laughed. I fell into the emotional reasoning trap, and believed everyone was thinking I was clumsy and stupid. In fact, my date was sympathetic. We went out for quite a while after that, so it wasn't the end of the world. I am more than one split-second awkward action. I survived. So will you.

What if I get drunk and do something I regret?

Dutch courage can cause problems. Here are some solutions. One is to drink a pint of milk and eat two slices of bread and butter before you go out. Another is to alternate alcoholic and non-alcoholic drinks. If you go to the bar yourself and never leave your drink unattended, you can be sure nobody's getting you loaded. Drinking competitions are a big mistake. A safe rule is to allow yourself one glass of wine, or a single shot of spirits, or half a pint of ordinary lager, cider or beer an hour. You don't have to have a drink just because the other person does, but do offer to buy a round when it's your turn! You don't need to be blotto before you speak – it's much better to build up your confidence instead.

Nameless dreads

For many people their last (or most memorable) experience of dating was that awful teen angst where you felt your whole life depended on someone else's impression of you. Those were the days when 'I've got a boyfriend' or 'I've scored with a girl' seemed like a passport to being cool. You've learned a lot since then. You no longer blur responsibility for your self-esteem by hanging it on someone else. You're in control enough to give yourself a treat. Do a centring exercise (see page 100) and rehearse the date as going fabulously well. See yourself being suave, sophisticated, attractive and witty. And make sure there's neither spinach nor lipstick on your teeth.

What if he stands me up?

Possibly he's late or he's had an accident. Then again, perhaps he's not going to turn up. That's why it's a good idea to meet inside where there's something to do. People won't automatically assume you've been stood up and that there's something wrong with you! Most people have been stood up at one time or another. Most people – if they gave it a thought, which they probably won't – would be sympathetic. If you have his phone number, you could ring. It's generally better than giving out your phone number or address until you know and trust him. My cut-off point was twenty minutes (and I started chatting with other people in the meantime). Some people's is as little as five. Being punctual – or at least communicating – is courteous. Standing you up is not. You're better off without them.

What if she wants sex?

Sex on a first date? You might decide this is the way you want to go. But I feel that in practical and emotional terms, it's usually a bad idea, and I'll tell you why in the next chapter. Unless, of course, you know you and the other person just want sex without the relationship.

Taking time off for good behaviour

Dating can be a strain. It's OK to ration yourself to just two or three events a week or a month. You're already building up your Wheel of Life and finding other paths to fulfilment. Pacing yourself isn't cowardice, it's good sense – your reward for being brave enough to overcome your dating nerves in the first place.

How can I keep myself safe?

Whether you're just starting to date, or getting back into the scene and need a reminder, here are a few simple but crucial safety rules:

- *Never meet someone you don't know really well in a dark or lonely place*, such as a car-park. Don't give them your address, don't let them come and pick you up, and don't go and pick them up. Meet them inside a public place that you know is open and brightly lit. Be specific: 'I'll see you at the bar in the lounge of the XXX Pub on YYY Street at 8 o'clock.' This saves trailing round looking for them.

- *Always tell a friend where you're going*, who you're going to meet and when you expect to be back. Make sure you call to say you're home safely.

- *Take a mobile phone* and call for help if you need it.

- *Go by taxi.* Even if you're a driver. This gives you a safe escort (so long as you know the cab company) and lets you be independent even if you get a bit squiffy. Which means first dates on Christmas Eve may not be such a bright idea. Spend holidays with friends or family, or curl up with a good book.

- *Only double-date if you know and trust at least one of the other people.*

- *Don't make your first few dates with him plus gangs of his mates.*

- *Don't expect someone you've just bumped into to give you their correct phone number.* Chalk it up to experience. It was probably self-protection on her part because she didn't know you well enough to trust you. At least you had some fun for an hour or so. And maybe it was the right number after all!

- *Don't expect people who say 'I'll call you' to call you.* If they say they'll call you on Wednesday at 7 o'clock, they're more likely to be reliable. It's OK to negotiate for a specific time. If they stay vague, be wary.

- *Dating is a numbers game.* The more you do it, the better your chances. First time lucky is probably not going to happen. Every frog you kiss gets you closer to your prince or princess. I've made some good friends on blind dates.

Where can I meet someone decent?

- *Network* through friends, colleagues, business associations and family.

- *Expand your Wheel of Life.* Go to things you enjoy and things you haven't tried before. It's OK to go on your own. When you get there, go up to someone else of your gender and ask, 'Do you mind if I join you?' They'll probably be glad of someone to talk to. You can always circulate when you've had a few minutes to observe things. For a while you may do more barndancing, hang-gliding or volunteering than you normally would, but that's OK. You're having some fun and maybe doing some good.

- *Use your library and local paper to check what's on.*

- *Social clubs* of all sorts could be what you're after.

- *Dating agencies* vary enormously in price and aren't always careful with their matching. People do get lucky, but I remember a barrister joining an agency for professionals and being matched with a professional carpet-layer. That wouldn't have mattered if the carpet-layer hadn't had homicidal fantasies . . .

- *Dating dances, dating dinners* and *lonely hearts columns* can all be fun. Try your local press – but stay safe (see the points above). And make sure you and your date can recognise each other. Descriptions are useful. Wearing a red carnation is an amusing cliché – or carry a magazine.

- *Singles clubs and holidays* are a great opportunity to practise your mingling skills, but again, remember to stay safe.

- *Interest holidays* can be good. Painting weekends, coach tours of Spanish castles – the choice is yours. You may find you're with people you don't fancy or who are not available, so don't go if you don't share the interest. And don't pretend you're an expert if you're not. People like teaching learners.

Summary
Dating is a numbers game. You have to be in it to win it. Confidence comes with practice, and with rehearsing positive fantasies of you acting naturally. Your self-esteem doesn't depend on the approval of strangers. Keep yourself safe. Building up your Wheel of Life is fun, and means you don't put all your eggs in the dating basket.

18

The Safe Pace

Have you ever found yourself diving in at the deep end only to come to grief? The Safe Pace is a way to maintain comfort and security with new people

Keeping yourself safe
You may feel that some of this chapter is blindingly obvious, but social mores are continually evolving. If, like a lot of my clients, you're nervous about dating again after a long break, you could find these ideas reassuring!

On the brink of a first date with someone new, you may be wondering about all sorts of things. How do you manage the first date so you feel comfortable? How soon do you bow out or fix another meeting? When do you know this relationship has potential? How soon is too soon for sex? Let's take it one question at a time.

The first date
If you walk in shoulders back and head high as you look around, you'll give the impression of confidence. After all, you have 50 per cent of the power in the situation and you have every right to be yourself and belong wherever you are.

A smile, a look in the person's eye and a firm handshake are good ways of starting. It helps to make the other person feel welcome and at ease. A sincere compliment ('I like your earrings/tie') goes down well but overdoing it seems insincere. Most people like to talk about themselves. Where they're from, what they think of their job and what they enjoy are good ice-breakers. Open-ended questions (ones that don't expect a yes/no answer) help keep the conversation flowing. It's not the Spanish Inquisition, though, so do talk about yourself too.

Keep things upbeat and cheerful. You want them to think you're interested and interesting, not a whinger. Watch the other person for signs that they're bored, and let them speak as well. You don't have to know everything. Silent Signals help you make a good first impression, though you might not want to be too flirty until you've worked out whether you want to take this further.

Another tip is mirroring: if you gradually match their posture with your own and then relax, they'll probably relax too. But it's important to be subtle about this!

After half an hour or so you can start finding out some of the other things you want to know. From around the age of thirty it's OK to ask, 'How come you're on the dating scene?', perhaps with a compliment thrown in. If you're asked the same question, a light-hearted answer is more welcoming than bitterness. With people from dating groups, it's fine to ask what they think of the agency, who else they've met and what aspects of dating they enjoy.

If you feel comfortable enough, you might ask her what sort of relationships she's interested in. That's relationships, plural. Someone you've met through a dating agency may have other people lined up. This is just a date, not the answer to all your prayers!

What about intimate kissing at the end of the first date? It's your call. It might not be a good idea yet, though, because it starts to make emotional connections you (or he!) may not be ready for. 'Thanks for a lovely evening' is a useful line, which you can follow with either: 'I don't think we'd suit but I did enjoy meeting you. Goodbye and good luck' or by fixing up a firm time for a telephone call or the next date. Nobody deserves to spend hours waiting by the phone. And since your Wheel of Life is rolling full tilt, you'll be too busy for vague suggestions.

Second and third dates

This is a good time to check out what he wants from a relationship. Again, Silent Signals give you a good indication of what he really thinks. If his answers don't fit in with what you want, there's not much point in going on. But you might become 'just good friends' to make outings more fun while you're both waiting for the person you really want.

It's important to sort out your ground rules so that you both know where you stand. Exclusivity is probably not going to happen at this point, and you might decide this is another good reason for not having sex just yet.

Please listen to your feelings. Your subconscious spots all sorts of clues that you're not consciously aware of. If you feel disregarded – and especially if you feel unsafe – why not finish with this person before you get in too deep?

If the person has earned your trust so far, you might decide – if you haven't already – to try a little intimate kissing round the end of the third date.

How often do we go out?

After the third date you may be starting to think this relationship might work out. As yet you won't know because there'll still be some element of 'best behaviour' on both sides. But it's still only *a* relationship, not necessarily *the* relationship. Expecting to see each other more than a couple of times a week is unrealistic – or it may indicate that the other person is hoping to pin a Hero mask on you.

Besides, you've got lots of other relationships going – with friends and possibly other dating partners. It's plain bad manners to drop them just because there's someone new on your scene.

After a couple of weeks you may want to introduce him to one or two of your friends. Their judgement can help give you more perspective on him, and you get to see how he behaves in a different social context. It needn't be a big deal; a visit to a bowling alley or some other casual gathering is fine. If he turns out to be an embarrassment, why not call it a day? And you'll probably want to meet some of his friends. A man is known by the company he keeps. The same is true of women. If her friends are raucous ladettes, she probably is too. If this is what you want, fine. If not, you can say your goodbyes before it all gets too serious.

After a month or so you may jointly decide whether this is going to be an exclusive relationship. If she's shown herself to be honest, reliable and open in other ways, and if you've both visited the other's home, there's enough evidence that you can place more trust in her. If your partner has young children, though, she may not want you to meet them until she knows whether this is going to be a serious relationship.

Once you've both decided on exclusivity, you'll probably want to up the number of times a week that you see him. If he's being cagey about this you may wonder why. It could be some practical reason – but it could be an unwillingness to develop intimacy. Let your feelings guide you. If you're getting a 'back off' message, feel free to back off so far you don't see him again!

The next step . . . making love
Obviously, deciding when or if you'll make love is a matter of personal taste. But there's a big element of self-protection here too.

Sex brings out all sorts of hormones and pheromones (chemicals of physical attraction), so that your body ends up with an agenda of its own. It may want you to have sex with someone who's not treating you well. Its urges may result in your feeling carried away.

Sex can cloud relationship issues so it makes sense to discuss sex before you start to do it. You may find this embarrassing but intimacy is not just physical, it's emotional too. Intimacy rests on trust. And shared perspectives. If your partner believes sex is merely a bodily function and you want to make love, maybe it's time to get out before you find yourself in too deep.

Knowing the other person's sexual history is important. This has nothing to do with being jealous of previous partners. After all, she's with you now. But it's vital to know whether she has HIV or other sexually transmitted diseases. By using barrier methods (condom, female condom or cap) you can protect yourself. You can't get HIV from kissing someone! But practising safe sex, which includes non-penetrative pleasures, is important to your future wellbeing. Decisions about contraception should be mutual – and resolved before you make love for the first time.

You can also say what you are and are not prepared to do. A partner may try to pressure you into doing something you dislike by calling you a prude or unadventurous. That doesn't mean you are. It means he's manipulative. He may say that if you won't do it his way he'll finish with you. Good. Now you have proof he's manipulative. Get out first! You don't have to get into a slanging match. It's OK just to say simply, 'I don't like you pressuring me. I've enjoyed our time together but I don't want to take this any further. Goodbye and good luck.'

Religious or cultural pressures may mean that some people are not prepared to have sex until after they're married. Or she may just hate sex. The clue is whether she enjoys such intimacies as kissing or light petting. If she doesn't, you might want to get out while you can. Assuming you too enjoy love-making, that is.

Signs that making love is probably OK

- You and your partner have let each other into your lives and homes.

- You respect each other's attitudes and values.

- You've checked you both want the same things out of life.

- He's been reliable, open and honest, and so have you.

- She's shown she values you and cares about your wellbeing.

- He's proved trustworthy.

- She's helped you out and accepted your help.

- He's taken care of you when you're sick, even if it's just a cold or headache, and vice versa.

- You've exchanged sexual histories and preferences and decided on contraception and protection.

- You share similar attitudes to love-making, fidelity, male and female roles and children.

The naked truth of love-making

I'm not talking about who puts what where. There are plenty of sex manuals for that. I'm talking about the act of sex as an indicator of whether this is a good relationship for you. People show themselves most clearly during sex.

Whether you're a beginner or experienced, you'll know the first few times with a new partner are often a little awkward. Not everyone will achieve orgasm. After a few weeks, if it's still not working between you there may be an irreconcilable emotional problem. Here are some character indicators:

- Is she a considerate or selfish lover?

- Do you both help each other to feel welcomed and unconcerned about spare tyres or bony bits?

- Is there emotional content as well as the physical act? (Assuming at least one of you wants that.)

- Is he able to reach orgasm with you face to face? (People who are reluctant to do this are not emotionally engaged with you but with something going on inside their heads. It's an indicator of serious problems with intimacy, confidence and emotional availability. If he says it'll be different when he's used to you, don't hold your breath. It probably won't be. He may say he used to be able to orgasm face to face – but that's not here and now, is it? Don't go by what they say, go by what they do.)

- Did she need sex aids, videos or erotica? This may be a laugh, or a help in staving off boredom years down the line, but how do you feel about it: valued or discounted? If the latter, your feelings are sending you a warning.

Time to leave or to stay?

Sometimes people duck out without warning after the first sexual encounter (although your pre-selection process and the Safe Pace will have minimised the chances of this). You may feel this is a rejection of you, but it's not. People who do this have emotional problems and you're better off without them. If you're the one who wants a one-night stand, it's only fair to discuss your point of view first.

If sex between you feels bad, you need to address your sexual hang-ups – jointly or individually. You may, however, simply decide that now's the time to leave.

What next?

Assuming you both enjoyed your love-making, you'll probably be sleeping together regularly soon. It's the sleeping part I'm talking about. Leaving toothbrushes and clean underwear at each others' places is a good sign – so long as it's not the only one!

Within three to six months you may well be spending more time together than apart and you'll have joint as well as individual lives. Around now is a reasonable time to decide whether this is love with a future. Go by what they do rather than what they say.

At some point between six and eighteen months you might reasonably think about moving in together, if that's what you both want. If she's not living in her home but she hangs onto it much beyond that, you may start to feel uneasy. People who need escape routes are thinking of escaping!

If the promised commitment hasn't happened within eighteen months, it probably won't. It could be time to cut your losses and start again. But you've had valuable practice in being yourself in relationships – and you've still got the rest of your Wheel of Life.

Summary

It's worth taking things reasonably slowly and keeping all your Wheel of Life going. Sex clouds the issue so you may want to hang on until you've got the trust and emotional sides sorted. Sex is a good indicator of character, too. People who haven't demonstrated commitment within twelve to eighteen months probably won't.

19

The Love Scope

If you've ever wondered whether this is love or infatuation, the Love Scope helps you work out the difference before it's too late

How do you feel?

Being in love is a great feeling. You feel energised, alive, tingly when you think of him. Just the thought of making love with him may send waves of pleasure through you – sometimes at the most inappropriate moments! You feel proud. The world looks brighter. You may go round with a big soppy grin on your face. You picture him mentally all the time, and you probably want to show off photos and lard your conversation with 'We did this' and 'He said that.' (Although turning into her echo and boring people with her opinions as though they were divine revelations isn't a good sign!) If you have to be apart, you may experience a sense of painful loss and you probably phone, text, write or email each other often until your joyful reunion.

The trouble is, both love and infatuation can give you these symptoms. This is because being the focus of someone's attention satisfies your hunger for attention and recognition. It's fulfilling in itself and frees up some of your energy for other tasks. That's why people say when they're in love they can move mountains.

So how do you tell whether this is the Real Thing or not? The **Love Scope** gives you the low-down.

Folk indicators
I've heard all sorts of suggestions for telling the difference between love and infatuation. For what they're worth, here are some of them. People say it's love if you could answer yes to these questions:

- Could I wash her dirty underwear?

- Could I face that chin/that nose/that tea-slurping for the rest of my life?

- Could I picture us still holding hands when we're eighty?

- Could I stay faithful to him even if he was unable to make love?

- Could I look after her if she was terminally ill?

- Could I still love him if he got really fat, thin or wrinkly?

- Is she the first person I want to tell about my triumphs and disasters?

These may give you some clues. But there are more accurate predictors.

How can you tell if it's infatuation?
Infatuation is viewing your partner without filtering out the fantasy elements. It's getting a lot of your good feelings about the relationship from the *rehearsal* stage, where you find your positive

stimulation more in picturing her saying and doing what you want than in what she *actually* says or does.

If you're infatuated with someone you may also blank out or excuse unpleasant behaviours. You might be reluctant to tell other people about what he's done, perhaps to the point of lying. Alternatively, you may discuss him obsessively with friends because talking to him solves nothing.

With infatuation, you may believe you have to think or worry about him constantly. This might be founded on a belief that without that mental contact he'll leave you, or you'll be unable to cope. On the other hand, it may be that out of your awareness you mistakenly believe that if you don't think about him all the time, it's not love.

If it's not viewed through a filter that blots out unpleasantness, infatuation is dramatic, with swooping highs and lows depending on how you think she feels about you at any given moment. Infatuation keeps you off-balance, and you feel hurt when her Angel mask slips.

With infatuation, joint plans will remain daydreams, or break down halfway through. While he may justify his unwillingness to carry things through into action, you'll feel let down, perhaps over trivia, but the feeling will be familiar and uncomfortable. Many people experience an unpleasant clenching in the stomach or chest with this.

Infatuation does not leave you feeling whole and respected for who you are. You may experience a strong and frequent panic that without her you'd die.

You may be unreasonably jealous or insecure and you probably don't feel OK about telling her because you don't think she'll be supportive. You probably don't feel fully welcomed into her life.

With infatuation you probably worry a lot whether you're good enough for him. You stay on your best behaviour for fear he'll leave you.

In short, infatuation feels neither healthy nor comfortable and you don't feel good about yourself unless she's actually showing you positive attention.

The Love Scope

The first and most important point is that with real love you both act on the belief that the relationship is as vital to your partner as it is to you. Notice that this is firmly in the *behaviour* part of your Cycle of Beliefs. People can say anything. Consistent behaviour to show that your partner respects, values and cherishes you is a much better indicator. Real love is constantly demonstrated. Even during arguments you know your partner loves you.

With real love your partner doesn't hold back, exclude you from parts of her life or keep secrets. Instead she welcomes you into it for mutual companionship in joys and sorrows. Or, indeed, in mundane tasks like emptying the bins.

With real love you and your partner will go through a stage of planning your future, your home, whether you'll have a family, how marvellous it's all going to be. Along with rosy daydreams you'll both be acting to carry out your plans, whether it's meeting for a night out, booking the wedding or saving up for a holiday together. You know you can rely on each other.

If you really love each other you'll each enjoy together time and apart time and you'll know that you can trust your partner while she's away from you. You won't want to betray her or do anything you'd be ashamed to tell her about.

You may think frequently about him but you won't be worried that not thinking about him means you don't love him, that he's going to leave you or that you're incapable of existing independently.

You'll experience a secure sense of belonging. You'll experience your partner's love as all-encompassing and you'll feel accepted, warts and all. Your love will be equally accepting of him. If you dislike the way he leaves toe-nail clippings on the floor, you'll feel OK telling him about this.

You'll feel she is at least as important to your life as you are. Though you may be afraid that something awful might happen to her you'll know that her love has strengthened you enough so that you could go on alone if you had to.

With real love you won't often feel let down. Nobody's perfect but you'll know she's doing her best for the both of you.

You'll feel happy or at least contented almost always when you think about him.

You'll feel relaxed and at ease with her.

You'll feel centred and at peace. You'll feel glad that you've reached your happy ending and will want it to last always.

Summary

With infatuation you're insecure and off-balance. With real love you're at peace with yourself, stable and relaxed with your partner. You feel accepted warts and all, and you accept your partner in the same way.

Together
At Last

From Singles to Couple

If you thought being together meant giving up yourself, here are some tools to make a supportive transition from singles to couple

Have relationships left you feeling isolated or invaded? The **Building Kit** lets you make the transition from singles to couple as smoothly as possible.

If you or your partner have felt disregarded, **OPERA** is a way of managing respect fairly for both partners.

Doubts about whether your partner loves you may have made relationships prickly. The **Love Exchange** can iron out your differences.

If trying to put across your point of view has been frustrating, the **Sense You're Born With** can make life easier.

The **Trap Map** helps you find and avoid relationship booby-traps which may have tripped you up before.

20

The Building Kit

Have past relationships left you feeling isolated or invaded? The Building Kit can help you make the transition from singles to couple as supportive as possible

What is togetherness?

You and your partner have decided to spend time together. Perhaps you've decided this is the life-bond you were hoping for. Alternatively, you may be having a trial run to see if it works out.

Now you have three aspects to consider: you, your partner and that embryonic entity, your relationship.

You have done a lot of personal work to build up your confidence and sense of identity. You've used your Personal Safety Zone to check whether *your partner* is a reasonable match. You've selected someone who expresses love in ways you like.

But as you'll know, good relationships take commitment and work from both sides. This part of the book will help you make *your relationship* the best it can be.

A couple is more than two singles together. It is each of you accounting for the other while respecting yourself. Accepting you have different needs and abilities. The whole is greater than the sum of its parts. It's a loving refuge for both partners, a place where you belong, a springboard for each of you to spread your wings with the other's help.

Now for the fine tuning.

Where do 'I' and 'you' end and 'we' begin?

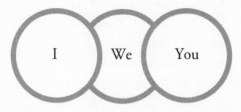

You and your partner are separate people. You don't blend into one great smear where you can't tell where you begin and end. Love is just the foundation. It takes time to build a relationship in the space between you.

So how can you build your sense of togetherness?

Transference and programming

It's quite common to forget your partner's needs and viewpoint from time to time. This is partly down to the fact that being with each other isn't a skill you've had time to practise much yet. But there is another side to it.

A mixture of *transference* and *programming* can prevent us from seeing our partners as they really are. In *transference*, you unconsciously see people from your past in your partner. You might even find yourself calling your love by someone else's name! The jigsaw puzzle image on page 118 is one way of representing this phenomenon.

Programming is all the automatic behaviours, thoughts and beliefs about your personal and gender-specific role that have built up in you over the years. Some programming is helpful – the way you make a cup of tea, for instance, which you absorbed while watching your gran do it. But some of your automatic programmed behaviours may upset your partner. It's an area where blind spots abound. But what actually happens when you act on transference and programming?

Beatrice and **Kevin** were happily living together as their wedding day approached. Then Kevin's father died unexpectedly. Bea bustled about organising death certificates and practicalities.

Bea assumed Kevin wanted hugs and someone to cope. Her first husband found it comforting when she held his genitals in a non-sexual way. So, exhausted after a strenuous day's organisation, that's what she did for Kevin. In bed, she reached out gently to hold his penis.

Incensed, Kevin called her a heartless bitch and stomped off to sleep on the couch. Confused and hurt, she followed him. He yelled, 'Dad's hardly cold but you don't even care!' Then he locked himself in the bathroom and wouldn't come out.

Bea loved Kevin and had offered him a combination of what she and her first husband would have wanted. In doing her best she'd wandered into mind-reading – and acted from both transference and programming.

What she didn't do was observe Kevin's reactions. If she did notice how he pulled away from hugs, she 'forgave' him because he was upset.

Bea acted out of love – but Kevin is not Bea. What she did hadn't felt like love to him. His marked reaction when she touched his penis was the first time she really noticed a problem.

In the throes of bereavement, Kevin found her touch demanding and inappropriate. He thought Bea didn't care. Over the following months he shut down emotionally whenever she was around. Bea felt unloved and rejected, so she tried cuddling up all the more to 'make' Kevin feel OK. Before long he was talking of postponing the wedding – when he was speaking to her at all.

Eventually Bea managed to persuade a reluctant Kevin to come to couples counselling. He wasn't convinced their relationship was worth saving – or that he'd had an input in their difficulties too.

So how do you establish – or re-establish – a sense of togetherness? As we'll see, you need to assemble a **Building Kit**.

The Building Kit

There are four tools in your Building Kit. *Observation* using all five senses tells you what's going on. Then, rather than jumping to hurtful conclusions, let *good faith* presume that your partner has a positive intention. *Communicating* – saying both how you feel and asking for information – lets you discover whether it was good faith or not. The hardest and most important part is to listen and accept the other's right to their point of view. Then you can decide whether you want to *adapt your behaviour*.

Here's how it went for Bea and Kevin. Without observation, good faith or communication, they'd both jumped to unfortunate conclusions and so acted in ways that hurt each other. Now, in counselling, they needed to observe, believe in each other's good faith, exchange information and decide whether to do something different. Here's how the dialogue went.

Bea: I offered practical help an expression of love and caring.

Kevin: For me, love and caring would have been you spending time crying for my father. I feel hurt and angry that you didn't.

Bea: I'm sorry you felt hurt and angry. I loved your father and wanted to show my love for you both by taking care of things.

Kevin: I accept that you wanted to show love. Are you willing to spend time sharing my feelings before acting?

Bea: Yes, but will you let me show love in my own way, by doing what needs to be done when you don't feel up to it?

Kevin: Yes, if you spend time sharing my feelings first.

One hurdle had been overcome. Here came the second:

Bea: I felt rejected when you wouldn't hug me back.

Kevin: I felt your hugs were demanding because I had no emotional energy left from my grief.

Bea: Do you accept that I hugged you because I thought that's what you wanted?

Kevin: When my mother hugged me it was to get something.

Bea: I'm not your mother. I wanted to give you comfort. Do you accept that?

Kevin: Yes.

Bea: When you pulled away I felt hurt and rejected. Are you willing to apologise?

Kevin: I'm sorry I hurt you but I was upset and needed some space.

Bea: Are you willing to tell me when you need space?

Kevin: Yes.

Bea: If I feel upset in future, are you willing to give me a hug?

Kevin: Yes, if you ask.

Two down, one to go – the biggest one.

Kevin (angrily): When you touched my penis I found it really selfish and intrusive.

Bea: I thought you'd find it comforting. Will you accept my apology?

Kevin (reluctant and unconvinced): Yes.

Bea: Do you accept that I was too tired after running round seeing the undertaker and everything to make love?

Kevin (hasn't completely accepted it): I suppose so.

Bea: Do you accept that I didn't want to make love when your father had just died?

Kevin (very quietly): Yes.

Bea: Do you accept that I only did it to comfort you?

Kevin (believing now): Yes.

Bea: When you locked yourself in the bathroom and wouldn't talk I didn't know what was going on and I was frightened.

Kevin: I was confused – hurt and confused. I thought you didn't love me or Dad. I didn't know what to say.

Bea: I do love you and I did love your dad. Are you willing to apologise for frightening me?

Kevin: I know you love me now. And Dad. I'm sorry I frightened you. I love you too.

Bea (in a small, scared voice): Do you want to stay with me?

Kevin: Yes.

At which point, he spontaneously hugged her while they both cried.

Using the Building Kit
Putting the Building Kit into effect outside the counselling room took practice. Bea and Kevin learned to observe each other and ask, 'How are you feeling? What do you want right

now?' It also helped when they explained why they'd done certain things.

They came to realise that what had seemed like the other's failure was also a strength. Kevin's sensitivity was an asset because henceforward he could use his emotions to ask for what he wanted. Bea's briskness was caring, not heartless, allowing her to deal with necessary chores in times of stress. She learned to ask Kevin what he wanted before she dived in willy-nilly. She began to express her emotions in words which allowed Kevin to feel accounted.

Summary

You, your partner and the relationship between you are all equally important. The Building Kit for your relationship holds *observation, good faith and communication* and offers you the choice of *adapting your behaviour.*

21

—

OPERA, the Respect Manager

If you or your partner have ever felt disregarded, here's a way of managing respect so it feels fair to both of you

The meaning of respect

I'm sure if anyone asked, you and your partner would say you respected each other. You would express admiration for the other's skills and personal qualities.

However, equal partnership means more than that. Although *equal* means *the same as* in mathematics, you and your partner may be equal but you're certainly not the same. Unless you're clones, one of you will be better at handling money, keeping your temper, being tidy, remembering birthdays ... That doesn't make one of you more important. Your relationship couldn't exist without the two of you. You're both equally important – and you have different resources.

But this doesn't always translate into true respect. Let's have a look at some of the areas where respect needs to be carried out in actions, not just words. Then you'll find a section on **OPERA**, a way of coping with those times when one partner's definition of respect doesn't fit the other's!

Where do you show respect?

Possessions and space

The space between you is partly physical. At home you presumably each have some cupboard space, space for your hygiene
things, a place for hobby stuff and so forth. There'll also be
common areas like the kitchen, hall and living room. If one of
you is obsessively tidy and the other is a compulsive slob, problems can arise. As can happen if one of you likes chintz and the
other hi-tech. Keeping your possessions in your personal space
and treating the other's possessions and space with respect makes
life smoother. Sharing decisions about common areas, ditto. It's
not 'Do as you would be done by.' It's find out – and do! – what
the other person wants with their things. She, of course, will be
doing the same for you.

Bodyclocks

Perhaps one of you is a lark who loves getting up bright and early,
while the other's a night-owl. This affects work schedules, meals,
bedtime and socialising. Bodyclocks are not about being awkward. They're just how our bodies work best. Having the TV on
loud when your partner's trying to sleep is behaving without
respect. Clattering around while the owlish one is groggy isn't
fair. In what ways does this bodyclock timetabling affect you and
your partner? Are there topics you need to discuss so that you can
arrive at a good working arrangement for both?

Love-making

A knock-on effect of the bodyclock syndrome can be the dispar-
ity of sexual urges. Men's internal plumbing means that bladder
pressure can lead to erotic desires first thing in the morning. Your
partner may not feel like sex until she's fully awake. If one of you
is having a crisis of confidence, he may not feel interested in sex

until he's sleepy enough for his inner critic to knock off for the night. Differences in libido and sexual preferences, particularly under stress, may feel like rejection or some other threat. Verbal rather than physical advances show respect. You can offer reassurance and explain if you're not in the mood, then negotiate for when you're both going to concentrate on your sexual relationship. On the subject of preferences, accusations like 'prude' and 'pervert' are counterproductive. Discussing and negotiating sexual approaches shows respect – and it's much more effective in getting what you want!

Money
Usually, conflicts over money arise when finances are tight. The anxiety often shows in arguments, particularly if you each have different levels of income. Having your own money is a big part of independence. It allows you to make choices. Between the ages when most people work – twenty to sixty-five – earning potential may be viewed as a source of self-esteem and low earning capacity as a drain on personal confidence. Money (or the lack of it) can therefore be used in less healthy relationships as a manipulative weapon.

You can account for each other's feelings and negotiate how you deal with money. My preference is for each partner to have their own bank account and then share a household account for savings, bills, holidays and so forth. Your preferences may be different. Negotiating what's fair doesn't always mean you pay in equal amounts. Nor does it necessarily mean that the one who earns most gets to spend more on herself. The criterion is: do you both believe it's fair?

Children and stepchildren
Providing you've both given up the silly 'love is a pie' theory that there's only so much attention to go around, children (yours, his,

or those you've had together) needn't be a source of jealousy between you. If you're feeling neglected, say so, and negotiate for more attention. A hug you get by asking is still a valid hug! On the other hand, children often believe that a parent paying attention to anyone else is 'stealing' the attention that 'should' be theirs. As a result, children may get into attention-seeking behaviours. Rivalry amongst siblings and step-siblings can cause friction. Also, children are often good at the divide-and-conquer approach, where if one parent tells them no, the other may say yes. Explaining what's going on to your partner as well as your kids makes sense! So does negotiating three-handed (kids and both partners) for attention, money, space and so on. Are there areas where you and your partner could run things more comfortably by making decisions together and, where possible, in advance?

Moods

Do you take out your bad moods on your partner, or cut off from her without explanation? While your mood is your own affair, how you carry it into the space between you concerns you both. Merely saying, 'Don't take it personally' is not useful. If you're yelling at someone, that's personal, whether you mean it to be or not. It helps if you can say something like, 'I'm in a bad mood because of work. Please leave me alone for half an hour to deal with it.' Or, 'I'm upset because my friend is ill. Will you give me a hug?'

Work

Sometimes a person may believe working long hours is an expression of love for his partner – but she might see this as a rival for attention. You can say how you feel. If one of you is offered a job that means a change of routine or even moving house, it's respectful to reach joint decisions about it. Timetabling, location of work and the allocation of domestic tasks can be agreed between you. Is there something here you and your partner could improve?

Chores

Women's liberation has shifted housework from housewifery to a shared role. In theory. In practice, particularly when one of you earns more money or stays at home to look after children, the sharing may be less than fair. The traditional division, where men put up shelves and women cook and clean, would be unfair if both partners work equal numbers of hours. Doing more than your fair share may be a manipulative plea for attention. It doesn't work and it leaves you feeling hard done by. Again, negotiating shows respect. So might getting a cleaner in!

Socialising

You and your partner will ideally have your own friends and interests as well as ones you share. However, one of you probably has more need for outside stimulation than the other. This can lead to jealousy and possessiveness, sexual or otherwise. Asking for reassurance when you need it is showing your partner respect. So is giving it! Discussing your social plans before committing to them means there'll be less friction. Is this an area you and your partner want to work on?

Time

Being in a relationship takes time. So do work, family, personal stuff, chores and sleep. It's easy to coast along not making time to be together. You can lose contact with your partner if you don't set aside regular time when you and she can go out together, talk over a meal on your own, or just snuggle up. Do you and your partner want to arrange a regular slot for the two of you? Even a couple of hours a week can make all the difference to your sense of partnership!

Privacy

Your partner may feel comfortable wandering around in her underwear and using the loo while you're in the bath. You may feel differently. It's a good idea to share your feelings and the reasons for them so that you can reach a compromise if necessary.

Are there other areas of disagreement between you? You'll know better than I do, but the way of managing them is the same: observe, share information with your partner about how you're both feeling and why, respect each other's right to opinions and ask for what you want.

Respect or disrespect?

Now let's get a bit less specific and examine people's general attitudes towards respect. Here you can get into real quagmires. Thinking you're doing the best thing for your partner isn't the same as knowing it! Here's an example of how this can break down for what seems like the best of reasons.

Earl was worried about his business because he had cash-flow problems. His partner **Nessa** was recovering from a miscarriage. They loved each other very much. For this reason Earl pretended nothing was wrong. He covered his anxiety by saying he was tired. The first Nessa knew of the difficulties was when the bailiffs came to take away some of their household possessions.

Earl's wish had been to protect Nessa. How Nessa felt about it was, 'You don't trust me. You don't respect me enough to think I can cope, or help you. You don't think I'm adult or important enough to tell me what's going on. You've lied to me so I can't trust you. You've shut me out of your life – so you can't love me.'

Nessa left Earl and went to live with friends. Earl, of course, found it harder to get back in balance after this double whammy.

So what do you do to ensure you're carrying both your self-respect and your mutual respect into the realm of action?

OPERA, the respect manager

Here's a simple five-point formula for treating yourself and your partner with respect – a summary of what we've covered so far. It's called OPERA, an acronym formed from the first word of each step.

- *Observe* yourself and your partner and act on the cues this gives you. If you're not sure what's going on, ask.

- *Pay respect* to your partner, accepting that she's an adult and has coping skills and resources you might not have. Trust her to come through for you.

- *Explain briefly* the situation that concerns you and how it's affecting you. This should ideally be summarised in just a sentence because nobody's brain is set up to deal with lots of separate points at once.

- *Recognise* that your partner has a perspective which is valid for him. For this reason you may need to compromise.

- *Ask* simply for what you want.

OPERA in action

Here's how it worked for Nessa and Earl.

Earl *observed* (better late than never!) that Nessa had cut off from him.

Rather than pestering her with phone calls she wouldn't answer, he sent her a letter with a bunch of flowers. He wrote that he loved her, he *paid respect* to her coping skills and was sorry not to have shown this before.

He *explained briefly* that he was worried because she was grieving and unwell and so he hadn't wanted to burden her with any anxieties about his cash-flow.

He *recognised* her point of view by saying he now understood how his well-meaning actions must have come across not as protection but as deceit.

He *asked* her if she was willing to tell him what she needed in order to trust him again.

The result was that Nessa agreed to meet him and then, eventually, to move back home. This time he allowed her free access to his business data. Nessa's income from her sales job initially helped keep them afloat. Then it turned out she had a better head for figures than he did, so she was able to help him regulate his accounts. Their marriage throve.

Summary

In every area of your life, remember OPERA: *observe, pay respect* to your partner's adult skills, *explain briefly* what's going on and how it's affecting you, *recognise* your partner's perspective and *ask* for what you want. Your partner may have resources you don't!

22

The Love Exchange

If you've ever doubted that your partner really loves you, the Love Exchange can iron out your differences

How do you know you're loved?

If you've jointly decided you're a couple, presumably you have both said at least once, 'I love you.' But it might not always feel that way. It's a question of you and your partner behaving in ways the other *recognises* as love.

Sadly, the ways people express their love don't always match, or happen at the same times. That can hurt. But if you show your hurt, you may fear – with some justification – that your partner will lash back at you or shut you out.

Have you ever doubted your partner's love because of something she does or doesn't do? Have you been afraid to say how you feel in case she cuts off from you?

Here's where the Love Exchange comes in handy.

What feels loving?

The way people express love varies enormously. In some families there'll be lots of cuddles and kisses between parents and children. They may frequently say, 'I love you.' These children grow up experiencing love as including a lot of physical contact. In other families where everyone keeps their distance, outings, treats and day-to-day care are supposed to be interpreted as love, though the message isn't always clear.

This means every single person has their own pre-programmed version of what loving behaviour is. So the way one person expresses love may not be recognised as such by their partner.

Differences in styles of loving

Joanna loves **Robin**, so she does his laundry, irons his clothes and cooks elaborate meals for him. However, she doesn't think he cares about her very much because he doesn't help her with official documents, which she finds confusing and scary. Also, he offers to help her with DIY but seldom makes the time. Robin, on the other hand, isn't sure where he stands with Joanna because she never kisses him hello or holds his hand in public. When he puts his arm around her, she goes stiff or pulls away. He feels hurt and rejected, so he's considering breaking off the relationship. What stops him is that she's passionate once they get to bed.

In every other respect, Joanna and Robin get on really well. They have similar attitudes about what's important to them, such as children, fidelity, background and money. They help each other with problems and each has let the other almost completely into their lives. Joanna and Robin love each other, but haven't quite made up their minds to live together.

Joanna came to counselling on her own, without telling Robin, because she was scared she was losing him. For her, this was a repeating pattern. She was giving herself a hard time because all her relationships had ended with her partner leaving. Being with Robin was the best relationship she'd ever had. Now it, too, was under threat.

What she wanted was something that would allow her to communicate with Robin in a way they would both understand.

Is this something you, too, would like? Do you want to feel more loved by your partner, and to let her feel more loved too?

The Love Exchange

This is one of the great tools from Emotional Literacy. Even when just one of you is interested in making changes, the **Love Exchange** can still get the job done. It's deceptively simple: just find as many ways of completing a sentence as you can.

You can work together on it. Some couples prefer to take turns in giving their ideas. The way I've found most effective with my clients is for each of them to complete the sentence in writing, finding as many endings as possible in three minutes. So what is the magic phrase of the Love Exchange?

I feel loved and valued when . . .

Joanna's answers were:

I feel loved and valued when someone cooks for me.
I feel loved and valued when someone helps me with DIY.
I feel loved and valued when people don't let me down.
I feel loved and valued when someone helps me with official forms.

Notice that *none* of Joanna's answers contained Robin's name. *None* of them were about touching, romantic words or gestures or physical contact of any sort. To me, *none* of them were obviously about emotion. Yet to Joanna they were expressions of being loved and valued.

I was intrigued by this, and it formed the basis of our next session. But for Joanna this was about a breakdown in communication between her and her partner, so in his absence I asked her to speculate what Robin's answers might be.

From various discussions and arguments she had many clues about how he might respond. She thought he would say:

I feel loved and valued when Joanna kisses me hello and goodbye.

I feel loved and valued when Joanna cuddles up to me on the sofa.

I feel loved and valued when Joanna holds my hand when we're out.

I feel loved and valued when Joanna cooks for me.

I feel loved and valued when Joanna and I make love.

As you can see, there was only one common topic with her and Robin's responses. I reflected back to her that cooking a meal might not seem like an expression of love to Robin. She was surprised that cooking for your partner isn't a universal symbol of love. Growing up in a poor one-parent family, she'd seen her hard-working father struggle to feed his children. When he served meals he would say, 'There you are, my lovelies,' the closest he ever came to expressing affection.

Joanna thought about it and still believed Robin viewed her cooking for him as an expression of love. However, we went on to consider the other assumptions she'd made about what he wanted. So far she had declined to ask him directly what he would need to feel she loved and valued him, but she decided to kiss him hello and goodbye every day for a week and see if it made any difference.

It did. Next session she reported back. With a mixture of pleasure and anxiety, she'd kissed him hello and goodbye six days out of the seven, and he'd seemed very pleased. She felt he wasn't retreating so fast. However, she had found it hard and told me, 'It felt wrong'. As with all her previous relationships she had kept a bit of herself back for protection because painful experience had shown that men always left her.

That tied in with using 'someone' instead of Robin's name.

I asked her if holding a bit of herself in reserve had actually kept her from heartache.

It hadn't.

Close to tears, Joanna started blaming herself for the break-up of all her relationships. Far from berating her, I congratulated her on a defence which had got her through this far. She and her brother had developed this strategy because their father sometimes went off for two or three days without warning. Working through this hurtful childhood scenario, she recalled a time when her father had come back and pushed his children away, sending them to bed without supper and shouting, 'If you don't leave me alone I won't come back next time!'

She'd been fifteen, her brother thirteen. After that they never hugged him again – but the don't-touch strategy didn't work because when she was waiting for her A-level results, her father left and she'd never seen him since.

For the first time, in the safety of the counselling room, she went from tears to anger and shouted all the things she'd always wanted to say to her father. Joanna also experienced great sadness and cried because her father hadn't shown her or her brother affection. She recognised that all fathers don't behave that way. Thinking of her married friends, she realised all men aren't cool and unreliable partners. She also discovered her power: when she pushed people away, they went away. If she had this much power she could use it to help keep people with her – if she wanted to.

With Robin, she wanted to. She now saw him, almost for the first time, as a separate person with different needs. She could decide – or not – to keep him at arm's length or let him fully into her life. She had choices.

One of her choices was to be more affectionate in ways he'd recognise as love. Robin responded well to this and she began to feel more secure with him. The following week she asked him outright what he wanted to feel loved and valued, and told him her needs too. Now more in touch with her own feelings, she became more aware of Robin. She'd chosen another busy man. But now that he knew it was important to her that he didn't make vague promises and that he did cook for her, he found time for chores, doing paperwork and sometimes prepared a meal!

Thanks to the Love Exchange, they're now happily settled and expecting their first child.

Working with the Love Exchange

You are now aware that different people express love in different ways. It's not that these ways are right or wrong. They're just different, and there are reasons for them. With your partner's cooperation you can use the Love Exchange by completing this sentence quickly in several ways:

I feel loved and valued when you . . .

Your may want to compromise or set limits. For example, you could say, 'I feel loved and valued when you cuddle me and stroke my hair.' You can't stroke hair all the time or you'd never get anything else done! So you could negotiate for her to do this on Sunday mornings in bed. In exchange you could get her a coffee and bring up the papers.

If your partner is unwilling to do the formal Love Exchange, you can use your powers of observation to find out what she wants to feel loved and valued. If you express your love in ways she finds nurturing she may be more ready to accept your requests in exchange. Sometimes you might have to carry out your side of the bargain for a week or two before she really responds but it's a step on the way towards getting more of what you want. Because you're being up-front rather than manipulative about your requests, you'll be protecting your self-esteem. You don't have to do anything that's repugnant to you.

Summary

You may not recognise your partner's behaviour as being loving when he intends it that way. It's OK to say, 'I feel loved and valued when you . . .', and to negotiate for how often you will each carry out the other's requests. The results of this Love Exchange can be dramatic!

23

—

The Sense You're Born With

If you've ever felt frustrated trying to put across your point of view, the Sense You're Born With can make life easier for you both

Why doesn't she understand?

Every couple has disagreements. It can be tempting to hammer on and on about a subject in the hope that eventually your partner will see it your way. You might think that if you can just give a few more examples, explain it again, shout it louder, they'll come around to your way of thinking.

They won't, you know. If you get into forceful repetitions the other person will probably feel threatened, invaded, rejected, hostile or scared. They may stomp off, sulk or shout back.

This can be particularly frustrating if it's something which affects your relationship. So how can you put your point across so neither of you feels hurt, aggrieved or just plain indifferent?

It's like he can't hear me

A common complaint is what the French call 'a dialogue of the deaf'. This is when neither of you really grasps what the other is talking about. Here's a typical example.

Don thought his partner **Liz** was silly to make such a fuss about his flirting with other women at parties. His argument was, 'But they see me go home with you, don't they?' He thought this proved to everyone – including Liz – that she was the most attractive woman in the room and he loved her. Liz felt neglected and threatened by his flirtations. They had endless rows about it. Liz would bring the subject up on the way to the next party, Don would respond angrily and say she made herself look daft, and they'd arrive out of tune with each other. Don now added a 'My girlfriend doesn't under-stand me' routine to his flirtations, thus eliciting sympathy from other women, who could see Liz glowering. After the party Don would leave with Liz but she'd be hostile for days, subconsciously hoping to punish him with her moods until he got the message. Eventually Liz stopped going to parties altogether and spent those evenings miserably wondering what Don was up to without her.

In counselling Liz explained this rather vengefully. She added, 'He just doesn't listen. He doesn't understand how upset it makes me.' Clearly she hoped I'd be on her side simply because I'm a woman too. She was also expecting Don finally to admit he was wrong when he heard her tell all this to another person.

Counselling doesn't work this way. The counsellor doesn't gang up on one of the couple, same sex or otherwise. It's about clients learning to communicate so that each understands the other's point of view. Whether they go along with it or not is a different matter, but once each understands what's at the bottom of their partner's complaint there's a basis for negotiation.

Do you and your partner have a subject on which you can't agree? Wouldn't you like a tool that gives you a better chance of putting your message across? Well, here it is: the **Sense You're Born With**.

The Sense You're Born With

People usually concentrate on the *content* of what you are saying. I invite you now to consider the *process* instead. This is a technique developed by practioners of neuro-linguistic programming, or NLP. Salesmen are trained to use it to persuade customers. In NLP terms, it's called matching representational systems.

People tend to experience the world in three ways: *seeing, hearing* and *feeling*. Even if all your senses function fully, you may receive information via one sense more than the others. You'll store and access data in your memory this way, and will express it most often using this sense.

Throughout this book I often use words such as 'you see', 'clearly' or 'looks like'. These words show that my main channel of information is visual. If I think of someone, it's generally a physical impression, mostly related to height and colour of hair. Only after that do I get round to adjectives like kind, aggressive or whatever.

These descriptive words show that my second channel of information is *feeling*. Many people say things like, 'I feel rough' or 'It's hard to do'. People whose primary information channel is feeling might refer to a difficult situation as a 'tight squeeze'. They'll describe something going smoothly, tell you one of their friends is a real soft touch or that their neighbour has a spiky personality. *Rough, hard, smoothly, soft, touch* and *spiky* are feeling words.

The third information channel is *hearing*. If your main channel of communication is hearing, you might describe a person as having a harsh voice or a loud tie. You may say your holiday was quiet or talk about the racket someone made. You might describe good ideas as sounding wonderful.

I don't tend to relate to the world much in terms of sound. Remembering examples of the hearing category was difficult for me because that's not my favoured channel. I have reasonable hearing and I love music and conversation, but my main channel of information remains visual.

Whichever channel you communicate in most of the time is the one you receive most communication in too. That's where you experience it, how you experience it and the way you remember it.

But your partner may not have the same main channel that you do. Which means that even if she can hear the words you are saying, they won't have the same impact for her as for you.

In order to get your point across, it helps if you first *listen* to your partner to spot their main channel. You won't have time to do this during arguments, so why not start practising your channel detecting now? Does your partner communicate mostly through feeling words, hearing words or seeing words? By the way, if you ask your partner what his main information channel is, he probably won't know. Likewise you almost certainly haven't realised up to now which one you use most, either. That's because people tend to concentrate on the content of communication, not the process.

Once you've worked out which channels are favoured by you and your partner, the next step in effective communication is to join your partner in his preferred channel and lead him from his to yours. In other words, concentrate on process. Let's *see* that in action.

Leading from one information channel to another
As you recall, Don and Liz kept arguing about Don's flirting with other women. Why not go back to 'It's like he can't hear me', above, and find the words that indicate which channels Don and Liz used?

Don communicated this way: "'They *see* me go home with you, don't they?'" He thought this proved she was the most *attractive* woman so people would *see* that he loved her. He told her she made herself *look* daft. His frequent *glances* at Liz showed her *facial expression* was *glowering*. All the words in italics are visual references. But what about Liz? She *felt neglected* and *threatened*. She *felt out of tune* with Don. She used *emotions* to communicate her *hurt*. Her main channel was feeling, with hearing as secondary.

In order to communicate clearly how she felt, Liz learned to use visual imagery. Don understood much better when she said, 'When people *see* you flirting with other women, it *looks* like you don't respect me. People *view* me as someone they should ignore because you do. What does it *look* like when people *watch* a husband talk to everyone but his wife? You *look* like you're getting ready to leave me and I don't like it.'

When Liz put her *feelings* into a *visual* representation, Don could *see clearly* what was going on for her. Now he understood why she didn't like his flirting. He'd always believed his behaviour flattered Liz but now he could *see* she didn't like it.

Don was quite cut off from his feelings, so realising that Liz's primary communication channel wasn't the same as his came as quite a revelation. It took him a while to become accustomed to this idea. He'd believed women were supposed to have emotions but men weren't.

To lead him into contact with his feelings, I asked Don – with Liz present – to imagine he was a fly on the wall, watching his human self flirt with a woman at a party. At first he described the woman ('pretty, but nowhere near as good-looking as my Lizzie'). I reminded him that that was what he'd seen as himself. What did he see when he became the fly on the wall and watched Don flirting?

His shoulders hunched. When I asked him about his tense reaction, he realised he felt uncomfortable and his stomach was tight. In his mind's eye he'd seen a man heading towards middle age, with a beer-belly, wrinkles and less hair than he'd like. He was upset that he was becoming old and less attractive. Responding visually to the world, he was worried that Liz would leave him, so he'd been trying to make himself more attractive in her eyes by showing her that other women valued him enough to flirt with him. This insecure aspect of his behaviour had surprised him.

At my suggestion, Liz invited him to take the fly-on-the-wall position again and to tell her how he felt when he looked at himself. The tight stomach, and the tension in his back, neck and shoulders, were the physical symptoms of his insecurity.

Once Liz told him that that was how she felt when he flirted with other women, Don decided to stop that behaviour and to spend most of his time at parties (he agreed on 80 per cent) with Liz. He also agreed to touch her frequently while they were out. He rehearsed ways of doing this that felt comfortable to both of them. They each offered reassurance in the other's primary channel. (Liz said, 'You *look* good and I like being *seen* with you,' to which Don replied, 'I *feel* good when people see you're my wife.')

As you can see (or hear, or sense), this technique helps build rapport and improves communication. Is there some aspect of your relationship which you could improve by using the Sense You're Born With?

Summary

Do you and your partner relate to the world mostly through *seeing, hearing* or *feeling?* Your choice of words reveals this. Expressing your point through your partner's main communication channel helps him relate to what you're saying. You then lead him back to your favoured channel so you have a precise basis for negotiation. It's just using the Sense You're Born With!

24

The Trap Map

Have unsuspected snags ever cropped up between you and your partner? Here's a map which can help you find and avoid relationship booby-traps

Hitting snags

Even when you and your partner love each other, life can throw you problems you didn't see coming or couldn't avoid. Relationship booby-traps aren't about the snags. They're about your reactions to them. And your partner's. Because sometimes the reaction is more damaging than the problem.

Under stress, either of you might respond in a way that's very different from your normal behaviour. Here are some clues as to what these responses might be, and how to handle them.

Rubber-bands

You and your partner might be well aligned in your general approach to life, but any human being's response to the world is not straightforward. In simple terms it is made up like this:

$$\text{Event} + \text{current abilities} + \text{support} +$$
$$\text{experiences} + \text{options} = \text{response}$$

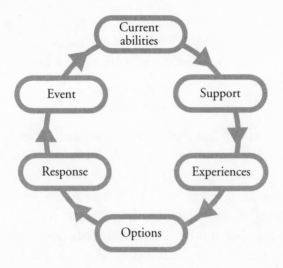

As your current abilities, support and early experiences combine to form your perception of the event, you and your partner could well see what's happening in very different terms. This doesn't make either of you right or wrong but it does affect your awareness of your options, which in turn affects your response. The response also feeds back and becomes an event in its own right. If an option turns out successfully, you will feel happier and more optimistic than if it doesn't.

A simple example might be a bill you can't immediately pay. When you and your partner see that brown envelope come through the door, chances are you won't both see it the same way. Let's see how **Henry,** a plumber on a building site, and his wife **Norma**, who's at home looking after their three children, respond when the electricity bill arrives.

Current abilities: Henry is already working as much overtime as he possibly can. Norma is exhausted looking after a fractious baby, an adventurous toddler and a son who needs a new school uniform. She can't cope with a job on top of all that.

Support: Henry and Norma are both tired, worried and stressed by the baby's crying. They each blame the other for not doing enough to help. Norma's parents have a low income and Henry has no relatives so they don't see themselves as having any outside support.

Experiences: Henry has come through difficult times before and believes they'll be all right in the end. His optimism is buoyed by having once won £750 on the pools. When Norma was eight her family was evicted and had to go into temporary accommodation where she didn't often see her dad. She remembers her mother crying helplessly and other children making fun of her because her hand-me-down clothes didn't fit. The humiliation she felt is still vivid, so she's never told Henry about this event.

Options: Henry hopes something will turn up before the final demand and thinks the best option is to ignore the bill until then. Norma is too overwhelmed by her childhood memories to think straight so she doesn't see any options at all.

Response: Norma internally replays the eviction scene, imagining her children will feel as bad as she did. She sobs and shouts blamefully at Henry, thus upsetting the baby and scaring the other children. Henry bawls, 'Now look what you've done!' and goes off to the pub. (In fact, he's gone to borrow some money from a friend. In case he doesn't get it he doesn't tell his wife, so she thinks he's selfishly spending money to drown his sorrows.) Norma feels alone, unloved, frightened and helpless. This becomes a new event and Norma feels it confirms her dread.

In transactional analysis terms, Norma's return to her childhood helplessness is called *rubber-banding*, as though she were on the end of an elastic band which snaps her back to that scene in times of stress. For a while it stops her functioning with her usual here-and-now reality awareness and skills.

When, later, she and her husband calm down enough, they will discover that they do have options. These include contacting a debt counsellor, arranging a budget account, sending a small payment on account, selling some possessions, borrowing money, buying a second-hand uniform from the school, and asking someone to babysit so she can catch up on her sleep. She and Henry can also discuss options for giving the other more support. If they had confided their basic fears *before* the event so that each knew where booby-traps might be, they could have solved the problem with much less pain.

Dealing with rubber-bands

If you experience rubber-banding, your partner may not understand what's going on for you. (In Norma's case, this was shame that she and the children would lose their home and what she perceives as their dignity.) Not explaining leaves booby-traps that trigger rows between you. If you say what's happening for you and why, your partner will usually be more sympathetic and, unless she's rubber-banding too, she'll probably come up with more options. By dealing with your emotions rather than bottling them up, they won't burst out in damaging ways.

In a rubber-band situation, there's almost certainly another survival emotion (anger, fear or sadness) at work. For Norma, it was anger at her parents for getting her into that situation. At the time she couldn't express her anger to her parents, whom she perceived as helpless victims. Now she's taking that anger out on Henry.

A more constructive solution would be to express her anger to her parents. In her imagination she could go back and tell them how she felt at the time. Their imaginary response would probably be how sorry they were, how much they love her and that they'd like to help her. Or, of course, she could talk to them in reality. Expressing your feelings and listening to imagined responses gives you a stronger sense of your current abilities.

A way of venting the adrenaline surge accompanying anger is to do something physical, like scrubbing or digging. Other people prefer a workout at the gym, or punching cushions. What about you?

Once you've dealt with your underlying emotion, you'll realise you're no longer a helpless child. You have options, which include asking someone else for options! You'll be able to ask for what you want emotionally. (In Norma's case, reassurance that Henry won't leave her to deal with the situation alone.)

Do you or your partner ever rubber-band? Are you willing to share your painful experiences in quiet moments before it happens? Will you both deal with the emotions in your rubber-bands so you can cut free from them quickly in times of crisis?

Other styles of response

In addition to rubber-bands, each of you also has an automatic response to stress. Unconsciously you may believe that this is the most effective or only possible way of responding to a crisis.

You may view your partner's reactions as unhelpful or even damaging. While you might say, 'That's silly! Do it this way instead!', he may not be able to take this in. This isn't being obstructive or stupid. It's just the way people are built.

Limiting options like this can add to the friction in times of trial, so let's find out how you can overcome the difficulties of such automatic responses.

Automatic adaptive responses

Remember that all responses come down to three choices: *thinking*, *feeling* and *behaving*, which tie into the underlying Cycle of

Beliefs. In the example above, Norma's stress reaction took her into *feeling* while Henry's was to go straight out and *do* something without thinking it through.

Another response to stress is *thinking*. This helps if you're able to tie it into feeling and behaving to make useful decisions. You probably remember a child in your class at school who thought something was too difficult, so he just gave up. He may have felt bad, or he may have started to play up, but he didn't work out a behaviour which helped him solve the problem because at times of stress he believed he couldn't think.

In any stressful situation you need access to all three areas of response. But stress can mean you minimise or cut one of them out. Norma's feelings were so overwhelming that she couldn't act. Her thinking was limited to, 'This always happens to me and I can't do anything about it.' Henry jumped straight into a behaviour which for a short time stopped him feeling bad or acknowledging his wife's feelings. He didn't pause to think that incurring further debt might cause longer-term problems.

Missing one of the response areas out means you don't get all the feedback you need to deal with the problem. It's not that you deliberately block yourself. It's just that for a while you don't have access to the other area of response.

This is why it's no good telling someone who's feeling down to 'snap out of it'. Her feelings hinder her thinking or behaviour. If his thinking's blocked, your partner can't take in your helpful suggestions. Getting angry with him will make it harder for him to think because his feeling circuits will go into overload. Nor can you make your partner feel something if his behaviour and thinking cut him off from his emotions.

These are called adaptive responses because in childhood, within the limitations of your view of yourself and the world, they helped you adapt to what was going on. Such survival strategies have got you through so far, but they restrict your chances of getting a better outcome – including the ability to work with the restrictions of your partner's adaptive responses!

So how can you widen your options? How can you and your partner contact all your adult resources of here-and-now thinking, feeling and acting?

Use all areas of response

Once again, the strategy is to contact your partner where he is and lead him into the other areas when he's ready.

For Henry, this would have meant asking Norma to talk about why she was so upset. By discussing her feelings and then contacting his own, he would have been joining her in her automatic adaptive response. With Henry's emotional support Norma wouldn't have felt so alone, frightened and angry. Able to access her thinking sooner, she could have helped Henry think through all their here-and-now options. Then he could have carried out a joint plan that didn't involve further debt. Working together would have strengthened Norma's thinking and behaviour so she was less anxious about future crises.

Now that you've seen how this works, are you aware of any situations where this can help you or your partner? Are you willing to contact her in her automatic adaptive response and then lead her into contact with her other areas of response? You will know when she's ready to move out of her adaptive response because she'll start responding in one of her other areas.

Results

By accepting and working from your partner's automatic adaptive response, you build a greater sense that there are two of you facing your problem with your combined resources. This deepens bonding and is the most effective way to deal with problems.

It was several years after the bill incident that Norma and Henry chose it as a representative example of their difficulties in problem-solving. As they re-enacted the scene, Norma told Henry about the rubber-band situation and they wept together. Norma no longer felt so alone. Henry now understood why she was so angry that he had left her sobbing while he borrowed more money. Eventually she talked to her parents about the eviction. They did indeed feel sorry and expressed how much they loved her. This allowed Norma not to stay stuck in feelings but to think and act more positively in crises. All this strengthened their love. When the next crisis came, understanding each other and pooling their resources was a joyful achievement for Norma and Henry.

Summary

In stressful situations you or your partner may rubber-band back to a previous crisis which limits your options for responding. Telling your partner in advance, or as soon as you can, about these rubber-band situations provides a map for avoiding booby-traps. It helps you respond appropriately to each other and the situation with all your joint resources. You can contact your partner in his adaptive response of feeling, thinking or behaving and lead him into the other areas so that together you can deal positively with difficulties.

Setting Limits

If you've ever felt your partner asks too much of you, it's useful to have tools that help you set limits

When you've had problems settling arguments, the **Win-Win Debate** can improve assertive communication.

If you've had a hard time staying out of arguments or dealing with criticism and sulks, **ERO** gives you handy ways of being heard.

Have you often found yourself giving in? Using the **Shield** gives you some practical ways of saying – and meaning – no.

Do you and your partner need a frictionless way of reaching joint decisions? Then the **Decision Maker** is what you've been looking for.

25

The Win-Win Debate

When you've had problems resolving difficulties with your partner, the Win-Win Debate can improve supportive communication

Differing attitudes to arguments

Partners can argue about everything from who stacks the dishwasher to where your favourite video's gone. The dishwasher might be the apparent subject of your debate but it's not necessarily what you're actually arguing about. Underneath, some other unresolved grievance lurks like an iceberg. Perhaps the anger from the current argument 'permits' you to air some other prickly issue. Before you know it you could be dragging up old 'sins' and carrying on like someone from a gangster movie. Your partner may prefer to: pretend nothing's wrong; apologise for everything since the Stone Age; sulk; mock; or slam out of the house.

If you're throwing so much ammunition, most of it is going to miss the target. You may not resolve the current quarrel and you could damage your relationship.

So what's the most effective and least painful way of arguing?

Three ways of arguing

An argument doesn't mean having a slanging match or throwing crockery! That would be *aggressive*, which might get you what you want in the short term but could destroy the foundations of your partnership. Behaving aggressively demonstrates a lack of respect for your partner and for yourself. It shows you don't believe you have any personal power unless you put the other person down, hurt him or leave him altogether! If you tolerate aggressive behaviour it will probably escalate.

Violence isn't the only form of aggression. Sarcasm, mocking your partner or belittling him, making cutting comments where he can overhear you, nagging, battering her with your moods or cutting off without an explanation all shade into emotional abuse. Aggression is not a sign of a healthy relationship.

At the other extreme is *passivity*. If you don't go along with your feelings to get what you need, that's passivity, which builds up anger, uncertainty and other unpleasant emotions. Passivity means giving away your power. Acting passively, perhaps pretending that you don't care or accepting the situation as 'just one of his little ways', erodes your self-esteem. Putting up with small things passively may invite your partner to get away with more and greater actions which will hurt you. You're not observing your own feelings or respecting your right to emotional and physical security. Nor are you respecting your partner because you're not presenting yourself honestly to him. Shielding your partner from the consequences of his behaviour is treating him like a child rather than respecting him as an adult, and it doesn't give him the supportive feedback we all need sometimes for social adjustment.

So if passivity and aggression don't work, what does?

The most effective course is to act *assertively*. This means you come from a position of mutual respect, a meeting of equals. You respect your partner's right to her opinions, feelings and preferences. You take responsibility for your own emotions and wellbeing without trampling over your partner or allowing her to use you as a doormat.

Assertiveness also means not taking responsibility for your partner's feelings or behaviour. Don't you cringe if a woman apologises for her husband's drunkenness? Or a man excuses his wife's rudeness because she's tense? Blurring responsibility is passive behaviour and erodes your self-worth.

Now let's concentrate on a healthy, assertive way to settle arguments.

The Win-Win Debate

This is a useful tool from emotional literacy. Because you (and I!) didn't necessarily grow up with this style of arguing, let's find out first what it's not.

The Win-Win Debate is not: shouting; making threats; nagging; name-calling; blaming; bullying; guilt-tripping; damaging property or people; taking revenge; raking up every subject under the sun; or inflicting your moods on your partner. All these are aggressive behaviours. You may know – or suffer from! – others.

The Win-Win Debate is not: accepting blame that isn't yours; taking responsibility that isn't yours; outwardly agreeing with your partner when you don't really; submitting reflexively to others' demands; pretending you don't mind when you do; lying; walking out; sulking; cutting off from your feelings; or any other tactic which doesn't help you act to get what you want. By the way, deliberately hurting yourself is passive. So are false cheerfulness, twitching, psychosomatic pains, and drowning your sorrows.

Most people have done at least some of these at one time or another. But from now on you may decide to do something different and more useful.

So how do you use the Win-Win Debate?

It's a simple three-part formula that's built on the following premise: *You respect yourself and your partner, you stick to the subject* and *you stay specific.*

The formula goes: *When (you) . . . I feel . . . so are you willing to . . . instead?*

Looks simple so far. But how do you apply it?

The Win-Win Debate in action

Lucy, a mother with a twilight-shift factory job, is arguing with her husband **Lee** about the amount of money he loses playing cards with his friends. In their circle, gambling is often perceived as a normal pastime for men and big bets are a sign of status.

Unfortunately, Lee isn't as good at cards as he thinks he is. Although he's not addicted to this pastime, he's reluctant to lose face by keeping his bets small. Nor does he want to stop playing cards altogether, as it's his main social outlet.

From her assertive position Lucy tries the Win-Win Debate for the first time one Saturday evening.

Lucy: When you play cards and lose, I'm afraid we won't be able to feed and clothe the children. Are you willing to give me a set sum for housekeeping every week and only play with what's left over?

Lee (defensively): I'll lose face if I can't make man-size bets. Besides, sometimes I win and you're happy then.

Lucy: I put 90 per cent of my wages into the housekeeping but I don't earn enough to pay all the bills. Are you willing to give me £250 for the food and bills every week and only play with what's left over?

Lee (aggressively): You blood-sucking leech! You want me to look stupid in front of my friends.

Lucy (calmly): My £100 plus your £250 is just enough to cover the bills. Your friends have families too. They'll understand. Are you willing to play with your extra money?

Lee (angrily): What about that dress you bought? A man can't have his bit of pleasure because his wife's stealing the money from under his nose!

Lucy (quietly): I pay bills with 90 per cent of my wages but when you play cards and lose I'm afraid we won't be able to feed and clothe the children. You earn good money. Are you willing to put £250 in every week and play with what you have left?

Lee insults her and slams out of the house. When he comes back at midnight, he kisses Lucy. Although he doesn't apologise, he does say he's talked to his friend Jack, who told him how worried he'd been about Lee losing money when he had a wife and children to support. Jack agreed that it's sensible to pay the bills first and gamble with what's left, a lesson Jack had learned by painful experience. In future, says Lee, he'll give Lucy the housekeeping every Friday after tea. If he wants to make big bets he'll save up for them.

Results

Lucy's first trial of the Win-Win Debate was a resounding success. Although she felt hurt by Lee's insults and manipulations, she didn't accept them as valid and so hadn't responded to them. By sticking to her point and offering a compromise she resolved an argument which had been dragging on ever since the children were born.

A few days later she raised another point.

Lucy: When you call me names I feel hurt and unloved. Are you willing to treat me with respect?

Lee (indignantly): That's not fair! I do respect you! I'm always telling the lads what a good mother you are, and what a fabulous cook!

Lucy: Yes, I'm sorry. You do often treat me with respect. I love the way that when we're in bed you ... (After a bit of giggling and smooching): When you call me nasty names I feel hurt and unloved. Are you willing just to call me Lucy when we're arguing?

Lee: I will if you will.

Problem solved – sort of. Unfortunately both Lucy and Lee had spent years yelling insults at each other so it took time for them to learn the new style of arguing and sometimes one or other would slip. All the same, Lucy reported that she and Lee were getting along much better.

How do you feel when rows get out of hand? Wouldn't you rather apply the Win-Win Debate to give yourself the best chance of getting what you want without hurting either of you?

Summary
Passivity, where you deny your feelings and desires, means you're unlikely to get what you want. Aggression may bring you short-term satisfaction but it breeds hostility. Assertiveness, where you respect yourself and your partner, is the most effective tactic and builds self-esteem. If you're specific and stick to your point, you'll have a good basis for negotiation and compromise. The formula of the Win-Win Debate is: *When (you) . . . I feel . . . so are you willing to . . . instead?*

26

ERO

If you've had a hard time staying out of arguments or dealing with sulks and criticism, ERO gives you handy ways of being heard

Staying out of arguments

The Win-Win Debate is great when you and your partner disagree. But wouldn't it be even better if you and your partner felt that most of the time you're not adversaries but friends? That you're both on the same side?

When might ERO be useful?

Sometimes, rather than arguing, you just feel out of sorts with one another. A bit niggly, isolated or even a little threatened. At times it can take just one word to find yourself at loggerheads. Low-level discontent might be expressed as grumbles or withdrawal. Alternatively, it could drag on with little outbursts of point-scoring, or it might erupt into a row. However it comes out, what you're feeling is uncomfortable. Here's an example.

Vic and his wife **Helen** were having a rare evening out without the children. They'd booked a table in a restaurant followed by tickets for a show and they were looking forward to it. Unfortunately, by the time Helen had dropped the kids off at her mother's they were running late. Both of them were getting prickly. At a red light Helen said crossly, 'We're late.'

Vic's response was, 'It's not my fault.'

True, but this response set them in separate camps. It was as though Helen's words carried a message of blame to Vic which he batted straight back at her. Suddenly they found themselves playing a tennis-game where the balls were emotional weapons.

When they finally got to the restaurant they didn't have time for the leisurely meal they'd planned. Helen said crossly, 'We'll have to miss out on the starter and dessert or we won't get in to see the first act.'

Vic answered, 'Well, don't look at me! I didn't make us late.'

Still true, but pretty much guaranteed to provoke Helen. Once again the unspoken blame had been batted between them and it had landed in Helen's court.

She bit her lip as they dashed off to the theatre but they spent the rest of evening sniping at each other. It wasn't anything major, but their hoped-for companionable evening was a disappointment to them both.

So what could they have done instead? In counselling they learned the ERO technique and replayed the above conversation differently so that each felt supported.

Have you ever needed a tool so that you and your partner feel not like adversaries but more like you're on the same side? If so, that tool is **ERO**.

ERO

ERO is an acronym of three words: *empathy*, *reflection* and *owning*.

Empathy is where you make contact with the emotion your partner is feeling. You don't have to apologise for things that aren't your fault. It doesn't matter if you don't feel the same. You just show that you understand.

Some phrases that show empathy are:

'I can see you're upset.'

'I'm sorry you're angry.' (Notice that this says you're sorry your partner's not feeling good but it doesn't imply any guilt, blame or responsibility.)

'You don't look happy and I'm unhappy too.'

'You seem tense. Are you?'

Expressing empathy, that is, acknowledging your partner's emotion, aligns you with your partner. It's even more uniting if you happen to be feeling the same emotion too.

By the way, you may not know what you're partner's feeling. In that case, ask! I've had cases where one partner said, 'You don't know how I'm feeling' and the other automatically replied, 'Yes I do.' That actually leaves the second person feeling unheard and discounted, and very often angry about that too. You're the expert on your feelings and your partner's the expert on hers. A better answer would be, 'Well, I can tell you're upset. Please tell me how you're feeling.'

Reflect back to your partner what it is you think they're upset about. This serves two functions. It allows you to check out what's happening for your partner and helps to align you mentally. Sometimes you can reflect and empathise simultaneously, like this:

I'm sorry you're worried because we're late. I am too.
Empathy ↑   Reflection ↑ More empathy ↑

Sometimes you may be mistaken about what's upsetting your partner. That's OK. You can't get things perfect every time! Whatever it is, she'll almost certainly tell you at this point, possibly in no uncertain terms. If you did get it wrong you can say, 'Sorry, I should have realised. It's because I'm upset/tense etc. too. Thanks for telling me.'

Owning your own feelings, thoughts and behaviour means you're aware of them *but* you're not assuming responsibility for other people's. If something is your fault, you can disarm him by admitting it and apologising. If it's not your fault, you can go back to reflecting, perhaps throwing a bit more empathy in. Some examples of this might be:

'Yes, it's horrible being so worried about being late, isn't it?'

'I hate feeling that way, don't you?'

'I feel awful when I'm late and I get in a tizz.'

Notice that with the two last sentences you've used the first person (*I* form) of the verb. While *you* can be a general word meaning anybody, your partner might take it as a specific reference to her and thus interpret it as criticism. The *I* form lets you own your own feelings and responsibilities and stay away from blame.

Sulking

Whether you get it right or wrong, sometimes your partner will sulk or cut off rather than telling you what he's upset about. You may be able to get back in touch by giving more empathy, perhaps saying something like, 'You do look awfully upset. I'm so sorry you're feeling that way.' A second apology and offer of reparation *if it was your fault* can defuse the tension. However, if your partner doesn't respond positively after more than one or two further empathising remarks, it's usually best to move on.

Sulking is a manipulation learned in childhood. Its object could be to get you to play caretaker and take responsibility for your partner's feelings. However, *you are not your partner's parent.* Your partner is the only one responsible for what he feels, does or thinks.

You may find yourself feeling bad or guilty because your partner's not happy. If you fall into the trap set by her sulking, you might end up doing something you don't want to because somehow you feel responsible for her emotions.

You're not. With adults you are only responsible for your own wellbeing and emotions. Unless, of course, you actually hit him.

Violence is the only time when anyone can legitimately say, 'You make me feel bad.' Hitting anyone is abuse and ultimately counterproductive.

So, if your partner goes on sulking even after you've empathised and reflected a couple of times, the sensible option is to own your own feelings and not hers. If it's something you need to apologise for, once you've apologised sincerely and made reparation if you choose to, that's it.

In practical terms, this means that you can stop feeling bad just because he feels bad. You don't have to stop talking just because he does. You can stay courteous, perhaps saying, 'I'm sorry you're feeling down so I'll leave you in peace.' Then you can go off and do something you enjoy, perhaps having a soothing bath or phoning your friends from another room. It's not good manners to gossip about your partner sulking – and it can have a nasty backlash if you do it where he might hear! If your partner's insecure you might add, 'I'm going to walk the dog (or other specific). I'll be back at seven o'clock.' That way you're empathising and reflecting again.

Now let's see how ERO worked for Vic and Helen.

ERO in practice

As you remember, Vic and Helen were niggling and sniping in an atmosphere of unspoken blame. As a result, they hadn't enjoyed their evening out.

Here's what happened when they replayed their conversation in counselling. I felt great hearing them and seeing their expressions. It was as though one of those cartoon lightbulbs had come on over their heads!

Helen: We're late.

Vic: Yes. You sound upset about it and I am too, especially after we'd worked and planned for our night out together.

Helen: It's amazing! I'm feeling understood and supported now, and warmer towards Vic.

They then went on to the hurried meal. This time the dialogue went as follows.

Helen: We'll have to miss out on the starter and dessert or we won't get in to see the first act.

Vic: Yes, isn't it a shame? But we could come back and have dessert afterwards if the restaurant's still open. Would you like that?

Helen: I'm really feeling like Vic can hear me at last. And isn't he nice and considerate?

Vic: I'm not feeling got at now. It's like we're on the same side again.

Quite spontaneously they got into practising ERO in all sorts of other little things that had been leaving them feeling antagonistic or isolated. I do like it when people carry on doing the therapy themselves!

ERO and criticism

Of course, it's quite common for couples to start arguing if one of them assumes the other is making personal critical remarks. With ERO, Vic and Helen learned to avoid such conflictive assumptions. But what if the criticism is out in the open?

Criticism can be hurtful. If it hooks into your innermost fears, you can end up responding to unspoken messages which may or may not be there. You might get defensive, go on the attack or swallow your hurt. All the same, both giving and taking criticism can consume huge amounts of emotional energy that would be better employed elsewhere. Let's see what you can add to ERO to deal constructively with open criticism.

Remember Steve, who updated his Cycle of Beliefs so he was no longer a lonely dot trapped in the middle of his Personal Safety Zone? (You'll find him on page 36.) He'd been wanting to move on from one-night stands to a full, intimate relationship, and within weeks that's just what he did. Over the next eighteen months he had different partners, each time getting nearer to what he wanted. He found that he and the third girl he went out with during this period, **Rona**, were a great fit. They bought a flat together – although he avoided discussing marriage.

Steve was, however, very prickly, and however gently Rona made criticisms, Steve found in them an unspoken message to which he would respond angrily. When they went on holiday, Steve insisted on driving despite Rona's apprehension. They got into the rental car. Before long the speedometer had touched eighty, and Rona sat clutching her seat, pressing invisible brake pedals. Steve was annoyed. Ninety. Ninety-five. Scared out of her wits, Rona said, 'Slow down! You're going too fast!'

Steve turned to shout at her, 'Don't be such a wimp! I know what I'm doing.' The car swerved and she shrieked, 'We'll be killed!' He went faster than ever 'to show her'. When they arrived at the hotel, miraculously in one piece, they had a huge slanging match. The holiday was a wash-out, and they came home early.

So what was going on? When Rona said, 'You're going too fast!', what Steve heard was the unspoken message: *You're stupid. You can't do anything right so I'm going to leave you.* This wasn't what Rona had said or meant, but it's what Steve took in. So he responded with defiance to block the message out. When he went faster still, Rona felt scared, angry and discounted, and that was when she started to think she'd have to leave him.

Steve rang me from his office to discuss what he saw as the end of another relationship, which was prompting his old fears to resurface. He was so upset that he was putting off going back home to Rona. We started with thought distortions. He was able to see that he'd been using emotional reasoning, but the whole thing was too close to home for him to disconnect its emotional impact entirely. I explained ERO and we role-played the conversation with him taking the part of Rona and me as Steve. I invited him to sit, move and speak the way Rona did so he could get into her character.

We got to the point where she said, 'We'll be killed!' Suddenly Steve realised that Rona's main feeling had been fear rather than condemnation – and that the fear had been painful for her. By looking at things from Rona's point of view – in other words, using *empathy* – he suddenly felt less attacked. Now he knew how unpleasant her fear had been for her, he was willing to apologise for frightening her and discounting her feelings. I asked him if he'd talk to Rona, using more empathy so he could check out what Rona was really thinking and feeling, and explain to her what he'd been feeling and thinking too. In other words, they would reflect back to each other what was going on, and only own their own feelings and actions rather than guessing at the other person's. Steve said he would.

He rang me back the next day, very relieved. The conversation had been difficult, but had worked out well once he'd started accounting rather than discounting her feelings, reflecting back to check what she was actually saying, and only owning his own thoughts instead of guessing at hers. A few weeks later he sent me a note and some flowers because using ERO had transformed his relationship and they were getting engaged.

Summary

Rather than feeling like you and your partner are on opposite sides, you can apply ERO to build rapport. Each of you is the expert on your own feelings. It's better to check it out than to guess. The Reality Key helps deal with unspoken messages. You can disarm criticism with empathy and apology if appropriate.

27

The Shield

Have you often found yourself giving in? The Shield offers you some practical ways of saying – and meaning – no

What does 'No' mean?

Those two little letters can cause far more grief than you might think possible. That's because people often load a huge amount of cargo onto the word *no*. Here are some of the meanings you might have thought are invested in the shortest English negative.

No, I don't love you. No, what you care about means nothing to me. No, you're on your own. No, I'm not good enough and neither are you. Or – *no* means *yes,* so long as I nag, wheedle or blackmail you enough.

For all these reasons, saying no can be hard. Meaning it can be harder still. When you add your own view of your position in your relationship, not to mention where you think your partner stands, you can see that some people treat *no* like an unexploded bomb.

But if you don't set limits, you run risks. You might end up working yourself to exhaustion. You might put up with being a dogsbody until you finally snap, have a huge row or walk out for good. If you've never expressed how you feel about tasks you've reluctantly undertaken, your partner might think you're suddenly making a fuss about nothing. You may lose your sense of identity and your self-esteem. Also, you might be letting your partner do something which puts you, her or someone else in danger.

There will still be times when you want to say no. If this has been difficult for you in the past, the **Shield** offers you some great tools for saying – and meaning – no. Following that are some guidelines on when to say no, but of course, if you respect your feelings and your partner's, you'll know!

Your Shield includes the right to say no

Your self-esteem is your Shield. If you value yourself and also trust your feelings, they can protect you. Respecting yourself as well as your partner adds to your confidence. It helps you say no.

Believing you're allowed to say no is the hardest part. This is something you can build up with practice.

Habits around saying no may carry two dangers. One is that you may not realise you automatically say no as a knee-jerk defence. A person with this defence may value her prickles because they get her out of doing things she doesn't like but in the long run it's going to damage her relationship and yours. Your feelings are your main guide but you can talk to exchange feedback. There may be circumstances you haven't factored into your calculations.

On the other hand, if you've lacked confidence in the past you may still tend to consider your partner as more important than yourself. An antidote is to realise that as half of the relationship, you have half the rights and privileges as well as half the obligations. If a lack of confidence has meant you've used manipulative ploys to gain your partner's attention, you may now realise that saying no will help defend you.

But you may not be familiar with effective techniques for putting your point across without alienating your partner. Here are some helpful tactics.

Address the unspoken messages

This is your first technique. When you talk to someone, you both tend to think that you're reacting to the actual words. In fact, you're more likely to be responding to the underlying psychological message. So it's very important to consider what unspoken messages you and your partner may, perhaps unwittingly, be bandying around.

Rather than getting specific about situations just yet, I invite you to consider whether what you or your partner may hear behind a no is actually there. Just because your partner is reluctant to iron your blouse, it doesn't mean he thinks ironing is women's work and therefore beneath him. Just because you'd rather microwave a frozen meal than cook a three-course dinner, it doesn't mean that you don't care about him.

Many of the unspoken messages *only exist in the mind of the hearer.* Perhaps in the examples above, your partner is scared of spoiling delicate fabric, and you're too tired to cook. The Reality Key made you aware of the thought distortion called emotional interpretation, through which imaginary unspoken messages cause you grief. If you're coming from a position of insecurity or uncertainty, this is an easy trap to fall into.

It helps, therefore, to address the unspoken message first. ERO works! You might say, 'When you said you wouldn't iron my blouse I felt unsupported. Will you give me a hug?' Or you could say, 'I do love you but I'm very tired. Is it OK if I just blitz us a micromeal or are you willing to make dinner tonight?'

Notice that the word 'no' didn't figure in either of these responses. Once you've got the unspoken messages out into plain sight, you may not need to say no. If you still want to, it will be easier now that it's not open to misinterpretation.

This will go a long way towards improving your communications, because at least you'll know what you are and are not talking about. Also, you'll have established empathy so that neither of you feels alienated. Can you think of times when you could usefully address the unspoken messages?

Other ways to say no

Some people need to learn how and when to say no. Knowing you need to learn this is the first stage in achieving your learning!

Timing

Is this a good time to say no? The first clue is in what you're feeling, but the main consideration is your safety. If you're safe, then saying no is an option. If you're not safe, what are you doing in this situation? How can you make yourself safe?

Beyond that, there's the question of consideration. If your partner is reeling from a massive shock, now is probably not the best time to start saying no. One man I know didn't think to cuddle his wife when her dog died. (By the way, the wife could have asked for what she wanted instead of expecting him to mind-read!) Although he didn't actually use the word no when he heard her crying in bed, he turned over and went to sleep. His wife felt rejected and belittled and thereafter became painfully aware of the other times when he hadn't shown empathy. Not long after, she divorced him. Timing is important! When things are back on an even keel, you can begin to practise saying no.

Start small

If you still want to say no when you've addressed the unspoken messages, you can start off with small things which are not likely to incur a heavy comeback. For example, you might not yet feel able to say, 'No, I'm not willing to do all the housework every week,' but you might feel all right about saying, 'No, I don't want to watch the ice-skating with you this afternoon.'

Some things aren't worth making a fuss about, but there's nothing wrong with compromise or making your partner happy *if you don't mind*. But if you're giving in and you feel bad about it, isn't it worth standing up for yourself?

Giving in unwillingly means you've made one or more of these decisions: (1) 'You're important and I'm not.' (2) 'What I want doesn't matter to me or you.' (3) 'I am willing for you to hear the word yes when I say the word no.' For your own sake as well as your partner's, it's worth starting to set limits.

I repeat, it can help to *start small*. If you've ended up watching so much skating that you feel like screaming, why not say no to part of it? You could say something like, 'I'll join you in ten minutes when I've rung my friend.' This doesn't even have the word no in it but it's still starting to draw the line. If necessary, you can repeat your reason. ('I'll enjoy watching the skating with you in a few minutes but I told my friend I'd ring her now.') As you've already offered your partner reassurance by addressing the unspoken message ('I'll feel abandoned if you don't share this activity with me'), you should have little trouble getting used to saying no in this or any repeating situation.

Permission to say no

If you're still having problems, you may need to ask permission to say no. If giving yourself permission doesn't seem to be enough, you can ask your friends or your family if they'd give you permission to say no. Everyone who cares about you and is personally strong enough will give this permission. Should you need it, you have my permission: it's OK for you to say no.

Rehearsal

Another useful tactic is *rehearsal*. First, imagine the situation in which you'd like to say no. Mentally picture it, hear it, sense it as clearly as you can. Then imagine yourself saying no. Imagine it being accepted. Imagine how good you'll feel for breaking out of your old acquiescent patterns and starting to set limits. Work through this as many times as you need to feel OK about saying no.

The second stage of rehearsal is saying the word 'no' aloud. Again, you may not feel able to say this to your partner just yet but that's all right. When you're rehearsing on your own you can start by whispering, 'No.' Then you can build up to normal speech, and possibly even to a shout! This is a physical release, but when you've completed your preparations you'll be able to say no, not aggressively nor passively, but assertively – because you have every right to say no when you want to. Let your self-esteem be your Shield!

The third stage of rehearsal could be to role-play the situation with a friend. You can have a lot of fun beforehand by getting your friend to go along with you in saying no to ridiculous requests. 'Will you climb Mount Everest before tea?' 'No!' 'Will you iron a frog?' 'No!' Then, when you get to the role-play of the actual situation, no will come more readily to you.

As with everything else, you'll get better at saying no with practice. Good luck with saying no!

Some ways to say no and mean it
Everyone can learn to say no with the least possible fall-out. It's best to stay assertive, rather than passive or aggressive. Here are some great ways to do that.

Saying no without saying no
Don't forget the Win-Win Debate formula: *When (you) . . . I feel . . . so are you willing to . . . instead?*

Empathise, offer an alternative and say no with a smile
This is a technique that's useful when dealing with your partner – and everyone else! Say your partner has asked you to take her suit to the cleaners. She's said she hasn't got time but you suspect it's

a ploy to get her out of doing this chore because she doesn't seem that busy.

When she makes her request, start off with some empathy along the lines of, 'I'm sorry you're pushed for time but I am too.' At which point you might smile, take her hand or make some other goodwill gesture. Then you can add, 'Are you willing to wear something else for now and take your suit to the cleaners at the weekend?'

If this doesn't get you what you want, you can move on to one of the following tactics.

The put-off

If your partner doesn't seem willing to take no for an answer, the put-off can be useful. You respond like this: 'I'm very sorry. I'd love to help you out but I'm really stretched right now too. I could perhaps make time at the weekend but that might be too late for you.' Or try something indefinite like, 'I'm really not sure. I might not be able to until the weekend. I'd like to help you but it might be quicker if you do it on your way home from work.' You can always soften the blow by making a conciliatory gesture, such as offering a cup of tea.

The broken record

This is a well-known tool from assertiveness training. It consists of giving the same message over and over again until the other person gives up. Said with empathy, it's effective – but only while you stick to your guns! Your response might go something like this: 'I'm sorry but I'm not willing to do that.' If you feel the need to throw in a little more empathy, you might say, 'I'm sorry you're so stressed but I'm not willing to do that.' A word to avoid here is 'can't' – unless you're physically unable to do something or you've never learned how! 'Can't' may be taken as weakness or helplessness. However much someone wheedles or guilt-trips you, if you keep repeating, '(I'm sorry but) I'm not willing to do that', sooner or later you'll get your point across.

Summary

Your self-esteem is your Shield. Saying no when it's appropriate is your right as a human being. If you respect your feelings and your partner's equally and you still want to say no, address the unspoken message first. Offer empathy and if you feel it's right, offer a compromise or conciliatory gesture. You can learn to say no by rehearsing and by starting with small matters. If you say no, mean it, and if you have to, keep saying it.

28

The Decision Maker

Do you and your partner need a frictionless way of reaching joint decisions? Then the Decision Maker is just what you've been looking for!

How do you make decisions?
Without realising it, you had your own strategies for making decisions when you were still single.

Now that you're part of a couple, your old strategies may clash. That means you might end up arguing over trivial things like who's going to wash the dishes tonight or what film you want to see. While even these issues can escalate into real strife, if you don't have a joint strategy for making major decisions, you could be in for battles that will leave you both scarred.

Perhaps you've acted on impulse without even thinking of consulting your partner. I know I've been guilty of this – even though I didn't like it when partners presented me with a *fait accompli* of their own! Ignoring your partner's wishes doesn't show you value him. If it's ever happened to you, you'll know what I mean.

On the other hand, you may have found it hard to make decisions. Perhaps you've shelved the problem, trying not to think about it, or spent a long time silently mulling things over. Perhaps

236

you've cut your partner out of the loop with some misguided sense of protecting her as though she were a helpless child. Not telling her why you were preoccupied would most likely have left her feeling excluded, which could have caused a whole new heap of sub-problems!

Some people are too easy-going to want the bother of making even minor decisions, too polite to 'impose' their will on their partner, or scared to take the responsibility. This becomes burdensome for the one who ends up having to make all the decisions, as well as meaning one of you doesn't get much of what you want. So it can build up resentment on both sides. Knowing what you want is good for you and good for your partner!

Another tactic you may have used is asking lots of people for their suggestions, perhaps coming back to your partner with, 'Well, that's what So-and-So thinks!' Again, your partner might have felt excluded, resentful and undervalued by the comparison.

The least helpful ways of getting your partner to do what you want are nagging, bullying and emotional blackmail. These set up resentment and put you and your partner on opposite sides so that 'scoring points' or 'winning' become almost as important as what the argument was about in the first place.

It follows that making decisions in a mutually supportive way is one of the things that makes you a viable couple. So could you use a good strategy for making joint decisions?

Reaching a joint strategy

Every new couple needs to spend time talking about how they are jointly going to run their relationship. Traditionally, when men were the breadwinners and the 'little woman' stayed at home, it was usually expected that what the man said went. If a woman had the final word, outsiders may have despised the man for letting himself be hen-pecked.

Fortunately, we now live in more enlightened times. All the

same, it's useful to discuss what you and your partner will do to reach joint decisions, because your approaches may be in conflict.

Not every couple will choose the same strategies. The **Decision Maker** works for my clients and for my husband and me. The key to minimising friction and future repercussions is to find a way that lets both partners feel they've been heard and valued.

However, the longer you've been on your own, the harder that can be. If you occasionally slip back into your old solo ways, as soon as you realise this it's time to 'fess up! A sincere apology, acknowledging how your partner feels and then jointly deciding what you're going to do next is a good way forward. I hereby apologise to my husband for all the times I've reflexively gone solo!

The Decision Maker

Points to consider when making decisions which will affect you both are:

Feeling: Your partner's feelings are as important as yours.

Thinking: You and your partner have different strengths and different areas of expertise. These double individual resources.

Behaving: Circumstances may not allow you to do what you'd like so you may both have to compromise.

The casting vote: If one of you feels particularly strongly about the subject under discussion, or will be more affected by the outcome, he might have the casting vote this time. Next time, isn't it your turn?

Notice that in this process the first point was *empathy*, so that both of you have expressed your own *feelings* and acknowledged the other's. The second point was *thinking together*. The third point was about *behaviour*, and the casting vote was back to *empathy*, that is, going with the strongest emotion.

A word or two about the strongest emotion: this is not about who shouts loudest or moans longest. If how you both feel has been heard and acknowledged, you won't have to make a big dramatic display. Histrionics are not a legitimate form of discussion! Acting up sends out messages that you believe you're powerless. It's a form of emotional blackmail. It will have repercussions, probably resentment and possibly fear, so it damages your sense of togetherness and maybe even your level of commitment to each other.

It's no use scaling up your feelings to get your own way all the time. Not only is this counterproductive, it can become downright silly. Escalating so you're practically faking broken bones in order to persuade your partner to make you a cup of tea will mean that when you are ill, she won't believe you. It's crying wolf and it damages your self-esteem.

What happens without the Decision Maker?

Here are two parallel case-histories. In one the Decision Maker was used. In the other, it wasn't. I'm giving you both so that you can compare the after-effects as well as the immediate results.

Renie had always wanted a houseful of children. Her husband **Stefan** didn't really like kids but he gave in for Renie – and because he wanted her to stay with him. He always assumed that after a couple of years she'd be back at work. After all, they had big bills and big dreams.

They'd taken on a large mortgage, Stefan thinking they needed a big house for prestige when he entertained his corporate clients. Renie had never told him she wanted the big house for lots of children. After the birth of the first baby, Stefan was often badtempered because he resented Renie paying attention to the child. Although he agreed to the second pregnancy, he was horrified when it was twins. He showed increasing resentment at being the sole breadwinner. After a while Renie was only happy when he was out at work and she was at home with the kids.

To keep the peace, she agreed that from now on she'd take the Pill, but she kept 'forgetting'. They had two more children. Now Renie and Stefan argued frequently. Increasingly stressed by supporting this big family, Stefan worked longer hours, then had an affair with his secretary. When Renie found out she hit him. Gradually she came to find comfort in vodka. Now that the precedent of violence had been set, Stefan would hit her too. Each blamed the other. Nobody was happy.

After an acrimonious divorce, Stefan sold the big house to pay maintenance. Shortly after his second payment fell due, Renie's bank bounced one of the cheques. Stefan had skipped the country, leaving her struggling with five kids, the bills and the bottle. It took her years to track him down and get a court settlement – whereupon he skipped again. The after-effects blighted the lives of not only Renie and Stefan, but their children too, well into adulthood.

The moral of this is twofold. First, if there's something you feel really strongly about, it's important to check out that your partner feels the same *before* you decide you're a couple. Secondly, decisions which affect you both should be mutually agreeable and then carried out honourably.

The Decision Maker in action

After a holiday romance blossomed, **Pablo** told **Georgette** he loved her. Though they'd only known each other a fortnight, Georgie loved him too. Pablo's first instinct was to propose immediately but Georgie said they needed to see if their relationship would work.

He was Catholic and his family was pressuring him to settle down and have lots of children. Georgie was strongly Protestant. She had a firm conviction that it was immoral to have more than two children because overpopulation is harmful to the environment. Also, she wanted to build a career in teaching, which would mean going to college. That would be difficult with a large family.

Notice as you read through the highlights of the conversation below that they both raise an issue and then respond with *empathy*, exchanging and acknowledging feelings. After that they *think* about it in practical terms, pooling their knowledge. They make suggestions of what they can *do* and decide on the solutions which they both *feel* best about. They break the problem down into small pieces and deal with one point at a time.

Where to live? Pablo didn't really want to live in England although he was prepared to do so for a while. Georgie was happy to settle in Spain because she loved the people, the country and the climate.

They both wanted children, but when to start a family? After a couple of years in which they could save for a home.

The crunch was: how many children? First they discussed their feelings about the number of children. Georgie said up front that this was an area on which she wasn't prepared to make concessions although she agreed Pablo had a right to a different opinion and she knew many Catholics opposed contraception. She asked him what he felt.

Pablo replied that he was rather startled because he'd always assumed he'd have a large family. Although he was a Catholic he said that many of his Catholic friends did practise contraception and he had no personal objection. In fact as Pablo talked about his feelings, he realised that it wasn't so much he who wanted a large family as his demanding mother. Recognising this, Pablo also added, 'But you wouldn't be marrying my mother.' Georgie had been about to make the same point. They laughed. They agreed that although Pablo would have liked three or four children, it was more important to him to be with Georgie. They would settle on two.

But what about working mothers? While Georgie would be

happy to stay at home while the children were small, once they were at school she wanted to go to teacher training college in Spain. She asked Pablo how he felt about his wife studying and then working.

He talked about his currently meagre income as a bank clerk and said, 'I like the idea of you working so that I have some help supporting my family.'

Georgie replied, 'I'd like us *both* to support *our* family. If you'll help with the chores and the childcare I can give private English lessons while they're little, and when I become a teacher I'll be able to earn much more.'

He told her that in Spain you don't apply to a school as you do in England. You apply to an authority which could send you hundreds of miles away. Her working could well mean that they had to move to another town, which would be an obstacle to his chances of promotion.

This was a thought that had never occurred to Georgie. She thanked him for his useful knowledge of Spanish life. Then she said, 'But aren't there international schools? Could I apply directly to one of them?'

This was a possibility. They decided to find out. Meantime Pablo would enquire about teacher training requirements and costs in Spain, and Georgie would learn more Spanish. They'd keep in touch by phone and email because it was coming to the end of Georgie's holiday. He would come over to see her at Christmas and she'd return next spring. That's when they would or wouldn't get engaged.

In the end Georgie and Pablo had a fabulous wedding in England that pleased her family. Pablo got a job in the Birmingham branch of his bank while Georgie went to an English college. They moved to Spain when she'd completed her teacher training, which also pleased his family. These were decisions with which they were both happy. This was seventeen years ago.

They're very happy together. Georgie is head of a department in an international school and Pablo is high up in a merchant bank. They have two lovely children and although Pablo's mother would still like them to have more, they're happy with their decision.

Opposition to the Decision Maker

Now some of you may be thinking that this is a cold-blooded way to conduct a relationship. Pablo's mother certainly thought it was!

But it was quite the reverse. Pablo and Georgie loved each other enough not to want the other to be unhappy. They would rather have allowed the other the chance to form a different relationship if that meant their beloved would be happier in the long run. At the same time they didn't want to stifle their own feelings, and they valued themselves enough to know that if this wasn't The One, there would be others.

Summary

One of the things that makes you a viable couple is including each other respectfully in reaching decisions. The Decision Maker is a strategy which begins with valuing your *feelings* and your partner's. You pool your combined *thinking* resources to decide what you're both going to *do*. After the feeling and thinking stages you again share how you both feel so that you can make compromises if necessary. *The casting vote* belongs to the one who feels most strongly, so long as this privilege isn't abused.

Sailing Off into the Sunset

Now that you're together, how can you both nurture your relationship and let it grow?

Good relationships

Isn't it funny how great romances like those of Mark Anthony and Cleopatra, or Romeo and Juliet, start full of passion and end in despair? I remember arguing this point with a divorced English professor who seemed to think great love had to be tragic. My summary was that people let bad relationships just happen, whereas good relationships are something you build. Saying I had no soul, she went back all starry-eyed to the vicarious ardour of her books. I went home to my husband. I knew which of us I'd rather be.

Lest I sound smug, I'll add that good relationships also have less than comfortable times. There are bound to be arguments and inescapable bad luck. There'll be stress and times of boredom or frustration. The difference is that loving partners can heal the breaches and help each other cope with hard times, and when the good times roll around, the couple can go back to being happy and contented.

Healthy relationships help both partners in being intimate *and* independent. Together you'll keep learning and growing. From the swoop of first passion to the excitement of dreams, the fulfilment of building your home (and family, if that's your joint choice) and then to the contentment of maturity, you'll allow each other support and space enough to enrich your lives and your love. Always you'll be aware that there are two of you, with different strengths, needs and perspectives.

In a good relationship your confidence in all areas grows. In a healthy one-to-one partnership, infidelity is extremely unlikely because you won't be tempted to break the trust and intimacy from which you derive so much pleasure. You'll be unwilling to practise deceit and you'll be free to express your emotions. In other words, you'll both be behaving in healthy ways and your closeness will deepen as, together, you deal with what is.

Sadly, death is inevitable. But in healthy relationships the death of one partner is less hurtful than in poor relationships. You might be afraid that real, involving, intimate love will make the pain of bereavement more terrible. It's true that open access to your emotions may make your grief deeper for a while than it might be where feelings remain buried. A lot of the pain of bereavement for the survivors of less healthy relationships is in helplessly wishing things had been different, rather than in acceptance of what is. *If only* keeps them prisoner.

On the other hand, if you're a survivor of an emotionally healthy couple, the free expression of your pain, fear and anger will allow you to work through these feelings more effectively so they don't fester or trap you. Also, the confidence you've enjoyed within your relationship will let you know that you can still find comfort in your happy memories. You'll have the strength to look after yourself and take pleasure where you can in other areas of life. You'll know, and appreciate, that your partner would want you to be happy. And, as a healthy individual, you'll have a network of friends and maybe relatives who will be there to support you. You'll know that a relationship, while rewarding, isn't the only thing in life, and that you still deserve happiness. You'll be able to deal with what is.

Part of the beauty of a rose is its transient nature. *Now* is the only time you can enjoy it. It's the same with a good relationship. Being aware of this allows you to make the most of your time together.

You'll both know that whatever goes wrong you'll act in good faith, wanting the other person's good as much as you want your own. Even when you're busy you'll make time for at least a smile and a kind gesture. You'll be looking forward to your time together and planning how to make the best of it, and meanwhile you'll be able to find fulfilment on your own.

You'll share your ideas and feelings and check out what's going on for your partner. You'll be interested in each other and in outside things besides. You'll request what you need and ask your partner what she needs, and you'll negotiate to decide what you're both willing to do. You'll be comfortable with agreed space and togetherness and you'll both feel valued.

Happy ever after

You may remember Cathy from the first chapter, who divorced her neglectful husband and found herself overwhelmed by lovey-dovey Jimmy. When she threw him out she was convinced she'd never get a decent partner and so was terribly upset. However, instead of leaving it to the fates she made some choices. You've seen that one of them was to change the way she thought. Jimmy didn't. He made two dramatic suicide bids to manipulate her into taking him back. When last Cathy heard, he'd done the same with his next partner – but he hadn't actually gone through with killing himself. He decided to stay stuck in his repeating patterns of behaviour.

It took Cathy a while to stop thinking she was a hopeless case and to learn to be cheerfully independent while acquiring relationship skills. Some time later she got in touch with me again. I was so inspired by what she said that I repeat it here:

'It took me four years and five attempts to pass my driving test but I kept right on going until I succeeded. Better than that, I've now got someone wonderful in my life and together we've gone from our L-plates to a brilliant relationship. All I needed was the right tools.'

Now you have good tools too. I hope you enjoy putting them into practice and finding maximum happiness and fulfilment.

Thanks for sharing this journey with me. Be good to yourself!

Resources

Books, articles and cassettes

The first list here is pitched more towards professionals, and the second more towards people seeking self-help books. But dip into both – you never know just which book might tell you precisely what you need to know!

Booklist 1: mainly for the professional

Andreas, S. and Faulkner, C. editors. *NLP: The New Technology of Achievement.* London: Nicholas Brealey, 1996.

Berne, Eric. *Principles of Group Treatment.* Oxford University Press, 1966.

Berne, Eric. *What Do You Say After You Say Hello?* New York: Grove Press, 1972.

Burns, David. *The Feeling Good Handbook.* New York: Plume/Penguin, 1990.

Erskine, R. and Zalcman, M. 'The Racket System', in *Transactional Analysis Journal*, volume 9, issue 1, 1979.

Goulding, R. and Goulding, M. 'Injunctions, Decisions and Redecisions', in *Transactional Analysis Journal*, volume 6, issue 1, 1976.

Grinder, John and Bandler, Richard. *The Structure of Magic II.* Palo Alto, California: Science & Behavior Books Inc., 1976.

Joines, Vann. 'Structural Diagrams of the Personality Adaptations Correlated with the Quadrants', in *Transactional Analysis Journal*, volume 18, page 88 (inspired by Kaplan, Capace and Clyde, 1984).

Kahler, Taibi. *Process Therapy in Brief.* Little Rock: Human Development Publications, 1979.

Steiner, Claude. *Scripts People Live.* New York: Grove Press, 1974.

Stewart, Ian and Joines, Vann. *TA Today.* Chapel Hill: Lifespace Publishing, 1987.

Stewart, Ian and Vann Joines, *Personality Adaptations,* Chapel Hill: Lifespace Publishing, 2002.

Stewart, Ian. *Transactional Analysis Counselling in Action.* London: Sage, 1989.

Stewart, Ian. *Developing Transactional Analysis Counselling.* London: Sage, 1996.

Ware, Paul. 'Personality Adaptations', in *Transactional Analysis Journal,* volume 13, issue 1, 1983.

Widdowson, Mark. *Affirmations: injunctions, permission and redecision.* TA UK 58, Autumn 2000.

Booklist 2: mainly for the general reader

Carnegie, Dale. *How to Enjoy Your Life and Your Job*. London: Vermilion, reprinted 1998.

Carter, Steven. *The Love Laws*. London: Piatkus, 2001.

de Angelis, Barbara. *Are You the One for Me?* London: HarperCollins, reprinted 1998.

Dickson, Anne. *A Woman in Your Own Right*. London: Quartet, 1982.

Forward, Susan with Buck, Craig. *Toxic Parents: Overcoming Their Hurtful Legacy and Reclaiming Your Life*. New York: Bantam, 1990.

Gawain, Shakti. *Creative Visualization*. Novato, California: New World Library,1995.

Gray, John. *Men Are from Mars, Women Are from Venus*. London: HarperCollins, 1993.

Jeffers, Susan. *Feel the Fear and Do It Anyway*. London: Century Hutchinson, 1987.

Lindenfield, Gael. *Assert Yourself.* New York: HarperPaperbacks, 1997.

Lindenfield, Gael. *The Positive Woman*. London: Thorsons/ HarperCollins, 1992.

Lindenfield, Gael. *Emotional Confidence*. London: Thorsons/ HarperCollins, 1997.

Lowndes, Leil. *How to Talk to Anyone*. London: Thorsons, 1999.

Norwood, Robin. *Women Who Love Too Much (and the men who love them)*. London: Arrow, 1986.

Redfield, James. *The Celestine Prophecy*. New York: Bantam, reprinted 1996.

Roet, Brian. *The Confidence to Be Yourself.* London: Piatkus, 1999.

Skynner, Robin and Cleese, John. *Life and How to Survive It*. London: Methuen, 1993.

Wilkes, Frances. *Intelligent Emotion*. London: Arrow, 1998.

Cassettes

de Angelis, Barbara. *Are You the One for Me?* Los Angeles: Audio Renaissance, 1992.

Gawain, Shakti. *Meditations with Shakti Gawain* (series of 4). London: New World Library, June 1997.

Goleman, Daniel. *Emotional Intelligence.* London: Thorsons Audio, 1997.

Hayes, Louise. *Loving Affirmations for Achieving and Maintaining Optimum Health,* Carlsbad, California: Hay House Audio, 1990.

Lindenfield, Gael. *Emotional Confidence.* London: Thorsons Audio, 1997.

McKenna, Paul. *Supreme Self-Confidence* (VHS video). New Hypnotherapy Series, Sony, 1999.

Helpful organisations

Phone numbers for local branches can be found through Directory Enquiries.

General

My pages: www.emotionalmagic.net;
   www.tiscali.co.uk/lifestyle/agonyaunt/askanne.html
UK Asian Women's Centre: 0121-523-4910
MIND (mental health charity): 020 8519 2122
PhAb (Physically Handicapped-Able Bodied): 020 8667 9443
Samaritans: 08457-909090

Physical/emotional abuse

SAFE (addresses domestic violence including towards men):
   www.dgp.utoronto/ca/~jade/safe/index.html
   www.womensaid.org.uk
Childline: 0800 1111
Incest Survivors: 01224 211079
MOVE (Men Overcoming Violence): 0161 434 7484
Parentline (for parents under stress): 0808 800 2222
Rape Crisis, central UK: 020 7916 5466
Women's Aid: 0117 977 1888

Substance abuse

Alcoholics Anonymous: 0121 212 0111;
  www.alcoholics-anonymous.org
Al-Anon, the support group for families of problem drinkers, can
  be reached through the AA number above
Aquarius (alcohol-related problems): 0121 632 4727
Families Anonymous (for friends and families of substance users):
  020 7498 4680; www.familiesanonymous.org
Lifeline (for substance users and their families): 0800 716701

Bereavement

http://griefnet.org
Cruse: 020 8940 4818
www.miscarriage.org.nz

Counselling organisations

Institute of Transactional Analysis: www.ita.org.uk;
admin@ita.org.uk (to find nearest Transactional Analysis counsellors)
British Association of Counsellors and Psychotherapists:
  www.bac.co.uk
United Kingdom Council of Psychotherapists (UKCP): 020
  7436 3002; www.psychotherapy.org.uk
Your GP may also be able to refer you to a counsellor

Gambling-related problems

Gamblers Anonymous: 020 7384 3040

Gender and sexuality-related questions
www.llgs.org.uk
www.gendys.mcmail.com
Beaumont Society (transvestism/transexuality): 01582 412220
Gay Switchboard: 0121 622 6589

Relationship counselling
Relate: 0121 643 1638; www.relate.org.uk

Single parents
Gingerbread: 0800 018 4318; www.gingerbread.org.uk

Single
National Federation of Solo Clubs: 02476 736 499;
www.federation-solo-clubs.co.uk